30
DAYS

A thirty-day practical introduction
to reading the Bible

Alpha

Published in North America by Alpha North America, 2275 Half
Day Road, Suite 185, Deerfield, IL 60015

© 1999 by Nicky Gumbel

This edition issued by special arrangement with Alpha
International, Holy Trinity Brompton, Brompton Road, London
SW7 1JA, UK

30 Days
by Nicky Gumbel

Originally published by KINGSWAY COMMUNICATIONS LTD,
Lottbridge Drove, Eastbourne, BN23 6NT, England

First printed by Alpha North America in 2003
Printed in the United States of America

Scripture in this publication is from the Holy Bible, New
International Version (NIV), Copyright 1973, 1978, 1984
International Bible Society, used by permission of Zondervan.
All rights reserved.

Illustrations by Charlie Mackesy

ISBN 978-1-938328-66-4

CONTENTS

HOW TO USE THIS BOOK   **5**

DAY 1   THE MOST   MATTHEW 28:1–10   **8**
             IMPORTANT QUESTION

DAY 2   EVIDENCE THAT DEMANDS   JOHN 5:31–47   **12**
             A VERDICT

DAY 3   IS CHRISTIANITY   LUKE 9:18–27   **16**
             A CRUTCH?

DAY 4   BE PREPARED   LUKE 12:13–21   **22**

DAY 5   EXCUSES   LUKE 14:15–24   **26**

DAY 6   THE DRAMA OF LIFE   LUKE 15:11–32   **32**

DAY 7   MID-LIFE CRISIS   LUKE 19:1–10   **38**

DAY 8   WHAT IS THE GOSPEL?   1 CORINTHIANS 15:1–11   **42**

DAY 9   KNOW WHAT YOU'VE GOT   EPHESIANS 1:15–23   **46**

DAY 10   RESCUED   EPHESIANS 2:1–10   **52**

DAY 11   THIS IS YOUR LIFE   JOHN 4:4–26   **56**

DAY 12   TRUE FREEDOM   JOHN 8:31–36   **60**

DAY 13   LIFE'S GREAT RIDDLE   ECCLESIASTES 1:12 – 2:11 **64**

DAY 14   WHAT SHALL I CHOOSE   JOSHUA 24:14–24   **68**
             TO LIVE FOR?

DAY 15   THE PURSUIT   1 PETER 1:3–9   **72**
             OF HAPPINESS

DAY 16   FREEDOM FROM ADDICTION   ROMANS 6:1–14   **76**

DAY 17	WHAT IS FAITH?	HEBREWS 11:23-29	80
DAY 18	HOW TO MAXIMISE YOUR POTENTIAL	MARK 4:1-20	84
DAY 19	RIGHT RELATIONSHIPS	JAMES 4:1-12	88
DAY 20	HOW CAN THE BIBLE BECOME A DELIGHT?	PSALM 1	92
DAY 21	DEALING WITH GUILT	PSALM 51	96
DAY 22	OVERCOMING FEAR	PSALM 91	100
DAY 23	SUCCESS	PROVERBS 16:1-9	104
DAY 24	FORGIVENESS	MATTHEW 18:21-35	108
DAY 25	LONELINESS	GENESIS 3:1-13	114
DAY 26	WHAT HAPPENS WHEN WE DIE?	1 THESSALONIANS 4:13 - 5:11	118
DAY 27	GOING THROUGH HARD TIMES	2 CORINTHIANS 1:3-11	122
DAY 28	PARADIGM SHIFT	COLOSSIANS 3:1-17	126
DAY 29	WHERE DO I FIT IN?	ACTS 2:42-47	130
DAY 30	'HOW MY LIFE WAS CHANGED'	ISAIAH 6:1-8	136

HOW TO USE THIS BOOK

The Bible is the most powerful book that has ever been written. It is a collection of sixty-six books, written in three languages and covering more than a thousand years. Although it was written by human beings over many years, God inspired it and speaks through it today. Studying the Bible not only illuminates our minds; it warms our hearts, feeds our souls and changes our lives.

The Bible often looks daunting, and it is difficult to know where to start. The purpose of *30 Days* is to help those who want to start reading the Bible. There are many ways to go about this. I have selected thirty passages which I have found particularly helpful. Some of the passages are from the Old Testament (which Jesus read and knew well), others are from the Gospels (which concern his life, teaching, death and resurrection) and the remainder are from the rest of the New Testament (mainly letters written by those close to Jesus).

TO GET THE MOST OUT OF THIS BOOK:

- Put aside time each day to be alone with God. A good way to begin is to pray as the Old Testament prophet Samuel prayed:

  'Speak lord, for your servant is listening'
  1 Samuel 3:9

- Read and think about the passage from the Bible for the day. Try and sense what God could be saying to you through the passage. Then read the comments that go with it, referring back to the passage as you go along. (The numbers in brackets refer to the chapter and verse numbers in the Bible.) After God has spoken to you through his word, then speak to him in prayer.

I find the following a great help in structuring my prayers. The order is easy to remember as the first letter of each section forms the word **ACTS**.

ADORATION   – praising God for who he is
and what he has done.

CONFESSION   – asking God's forgiveness for
anything that we have done wrong.

THANKSGIVING – for health, family,
friends, and so on.

SUPPLICATION   – praying for ourselves, for our friends
and for others.

Getting to know God is the purpose for which we were made. In order to do this we need to spend time speaking to him and letting him speak to us. Jesus himself set us a great example. Time alone with God has been the key for all the great men and women of God. From Moses to Mother Teresa, from the apostle Paul to Billy Graham. The prophet said,

'He wakens me morning by morning, wakens my ear to listen like one being taught.'
Isaiah 50:4

God has given us the extraordinary privilege of knowing him. I hope that by the end of *30 Days* you will want to make spending time with God – speaking to him and letting him speak to you – a lifetime habit.

30
DAYS

THE MOST IMPORTANT QUESTION

MATTHEW 28:1-10

The Guard at the Tomb

62The next day, the one after Preparation Day, the chief priests and the Pharisees went to Pilate. 63"Sir," they said, "we remember that while he was still alive that deceiver said, 'After three days I will rise again.' 64So give the order for the tomb to be made secure until the third day. Otherwise, his disciples may come and steal the body and tell the people that he has been raised from the dead. This last deception will be worse than the first."

65"Take a guard," Pilate answered. "Go, make the tomb as secure as you know how." 66So they went and made the tomb secure by putting a seal on the stone and posting the guard.

The Resurrection

28 After the Sabbath, at dawn on the first day of the week, Mary Magdalene and the other Mary went to look at the tomb.

2There was a violent earthquake, for an angel of the Lord came down from heaven and, going to the tomb, rolled back the stone and sat on it. 3His appearance was like lightning, and his clothes were white as snow. 4The guards were so afraid of him that they shook and became like dead men.

5The angel said to the women, "Do not be afraid, for I know that you are looking for Jesus, who was crucified. 6He is not here; he has risen, just as he said. Come and see the place where he lay. 7Then go quickly and tell his disciples: 'He has risen from the dead and is going ahead of you into Galilee. There you will see him.' Now I have told you."

8So the women hurried away from the tomb, afraid yet filled with joy, and ran to tell his disciples. 9Suddenly Jesus met them. "Greetings," he said. They came to him and clasped his feet and worshipped him. 10Then Jesus said to them, "Do not be afraid. Go and tell my brothers to go to Galilee; there they will see me."

The Guards' Report

11While the women were on their way, some of the guards went into the city and reported to the chief priests everything that had happened. 12when the chief priests had met with the elders and devised a plan, they gave the soldiers a large sum of money, 13telling them, "You are to say, 'His disciples came during the night and stole him away while we were asleep.' 14If this report gets to the governor, we will satisfy him and keep you out of trouble." 15So the soldiers took the money and did as they were instructed. And this story has been widely circulated among the Jews to this very day.

The Great Commission

16Then the eleven disciples went to Galilee, to the mountain where Jesus had told them to go. 17When they saw him, they worshipped him; but some doubted. 18Then Jesus came to them and said, "All authority in heaven and on earth has been given to me. 19Therefore go and make disciples of all nations, baptising them in the name of the Father and of the Son and of the Holy Spirit, 20and teaching them to obey everything I have commanded you. And surely I am with you always, to the very end of the age."

If you could meet any person from the past and ask just one question, who would you meet and what would you ask? When he was asked this, Professor C. E. M. Joad, then Professor of Philosophy at London University and a well-known agnostic, answered: 'I would meet Jesus Christ and ask him the most important question in all the world – did you or did you not rise from the dead?'

Either Jesus is alive now and we can know him or he is not and we cannot. What is the evidence that Jesus is alive?

1. THE ABSENCE OF JESUS FROM THE TOMB

When Mary Magdalene and the other Mary went to look at the tomb they found the tombstone rolled away. They were told to go and see 'the place where he lay' (v. 6) so that they could witness the fact that he was no longer there.

Women were not allowed to be witnesses in court in those days. If this had been invented by the early Christians, they would never have chosen women to be the first witnesses, so the fact that Matthew records the women's role gives the account an authentic ring.

2. THE PRESENCE OF JESUS WITH THE DISCIPLES

These women actually saw Jesus. They met him (v. 9) and he spoke to them. They 'clasped his feet and worshipped him' (v. 9). Later on, many others saw Jesus (Matthew 28:16–20; Luke 24:36–51; John 21; 1 Corinthians 15:1–8). More than 500 people saw him on eleven different occasions over a period of six weeks.

3. THE BIRTH AND GROWTH OF THE CHRISTIAN CHURCH

These women were utterly changed. They must have been devastated by Jesus' death but they were 'filled with joy' (v. 8). They rushed off to spread the good news (v. 10). Nothing other than the physical resurrection of Jesus can explain the utter transformation of Mary Magdalene and the other Mary, and then of the disciples, which resulted in the explosive growth of the church.

4. THE EXPERIENCE OF CHRISTIANS DOWN THE AGES

These two women were the first to experience an encounter with the risen Jesus Christ. Since that day countless millions of Christians have had the same experience. C. S. Lewis wrote, 'A Christian believes in Jesus not because he finds him by laboratory methods, but by actual contact with him. A Christian is something like the electric eel, which knows more about electricity than all the electrical engineers put together.'

It was on the basis of all this evidence that Professor Joad came to faith in Jesus Christ in the last years of his life. His final book in which he outlined his new-found faith was called *Recovery of Belief.*

The implications of the resurrection are far-reaching. Dwell on these three extraordinary facts.

You can be sure about the past

God raised Jesus from the dead. You can therefore be sure that the cross was effective and forgiveness is possible.

You can be sure about the future

You can be sure that if you have put your faith in Christ, one day you too will rise from the dead just as he did. Death is a defeated tyrant. There is nothing that can ultimately harm us.

You can be sure about the present

You can be sure that Jesus is alive today. He is near you right now. You can hear this same person speak to you (primarily through the Bible) and you can speak to him (as you pray).

🖐 PRAY

You might like to thank God today for the resurrection of Jesus.
Thank him that it is possible to have the assurance and forgiveness,
a secure future and the presence of Jesus with you each day.

EVIDENCE THAT DEMANDS A VERDICT

JOHN 5:31-47

²¹For just as the Father raises the dead and gives them life, even so the Son gives life to whom he is pleased to give it. ²²Moreover, the Father judges no-one, but has entrusted all judgment to the Son, ²³that all may honour the Son just as they honour the Father. Whoever does not honour the Son does not honour the Father, who sent him.

²⁴"I tell you the truth, those who hear my word and believe him who sent me have eternal life and will not be condemned; they have crossed over from death to life. ²⁵I tell you the truth, a time is coming and has now come when the dead will hear the voice of the Son of God and those who hear will live. ²⁶For as the Father has life in himself, so he has granted the Son to have life in himself. ²⁷And he has given him authority to judge because he is the Son of Man.

²⁸"Do not be amazed at this, for a time is coming when all who are in their graves will hear his voice ²⁹and come out those who have done good will rise to live, and those who have done evil will rise to be condemned. ³⁰By myself I can do nothing; I judge only as I hear, and my judgment is just, for I seek not to please myself but him who sent me.

Testimonies About Jesus

³¹"If I testify about myself, my testimony is not valid. ³²There is another who testifies in my favour, and I know that his testimony about me is valid.

³³"You have sent to John and he has testified to the truth. ³⁴Not that I accept human testimony; but I mention it that you may be saved. ³⁵John was a lamp that burned and gave light, and you chose for a time to enjoy his light.

³⁶"I have testimony weightier than that of John. For the very work that the Father has given me to finish, and which I am doing, testifies that the Father has sent me. ³⁷And the Father who sent me has himself testified concerning me. You have never heard his voice nor seen his form, ³⁸nor does his word dwell in you, for you do not believe the one he sent. ³⁹You diligently study the Scriptures because you think that by them you possess eternal life. These are the Scriptures that testify about me, ⁴⁰yet you refuse to come to me to have life.

⁴¹"I do not accept human praise, ⁴²but I know you. I know that you do not have the love of God in your hearts. ⁴³I have come in my Father's name, and you do not accept me; but if others come in their own names, you will accept them. ⁴⁴How can you believe if you accept praise from one another, yet make no effort to obtain the praise that comes from the only God?

⁴⁵"But do not think I will accuse you before the Father. Your accuser is Moses, on whom your hopes are set. ⁴⁶If you believed Moses, you would believe me, for he wrote about me. ⁴⁷But since you do not believe what he wrote, how are you going to believe what I say?"

Jesus Feeds the Five Thousand

6 Some time after this, Jesus crossed to the far shore of the Sea of Galilee (that is, the Sea of Tiberias), ²and a great

How do we know that Christianity is true? Jesus made some astonishing claims: earlier in this chapter in verse 18, 'he was even calling God his own Father, making himself equal with God'. But Jesus says his own testimony is not enough (v. 31). Supporting evidence is required. God the Father has supplied this evidence (v. 32) through at least four witnesses.

1. THE EVIDENCE OF OTHER PEOPLE (V. 33)

John the Baptist had provided supporting evidence. Earlier in the Gospel John tells us that 'There came a man who was sent from God; his name was John. He came as a witness to testify concerning that light... He himself was not the light; he came only as a witness to the light' (John 1:6–8).

Today there are millions of Christians all over the world, more than ever before, pointing to Jesus Christ. They come from every race, class, colour and background. They say that Jesus has changed their lives. He is the 'Lamb of God, who takes away the sin of the world' (John 1:29).

2. THE EVIDENCE OF THE LIFE'S WORK OF JESUS (V. 36)

Jesus says that 'the very work that the Father has given me to finish, and which I am doing, testifies that the Father has sent me' (v. 36). This evidence Jesus describes as 'weightier than that of John' (v. 36). Jesus is, as a former Archbishop of Canterbury William Temple put it, referring to 'the whole activity of the word made flesh'. Jesus' life's work includes his miracles, which were openly acknowledged to have happened at the time although some simply attributed them to demonic powers. The evidence also includes his way of life, his attitude to other people, the effect of his teaching, his influence on those who met him and supremely his death. Jesus said the purpose for which he was sent by the Father was to die for us ('The very work that the Father has given me to finish', v. 36). When it was completed, he cried out, 'It is finished' (John 19:30).

3. THE EVIDENCE OF THE FATHER'S DIRECT TESTIMONY (VV. 37-38)

First, there was the outward voice that testified directly at Jesus' baptism, declaring 'You are my Son, whom I love' (Mark 1:11). Second, there are the inner words of the Father, who speaks to our hearts and consciences (John 15:26). Third, the main way in the New Testament that the Father directly testifies is by raising his Son from the dead (see Acts 2:24).

4. THE EVIDENCE OF THE SCRIPTURES (VV. 38-39)

Jesus says, 'The Scriptures... testify about me' (v. 39). The whole Old Testament reflects Jesus – 'Moses... wrote about me' (v. 46). As the reformer Martin Luther put it: 'every word rings of Christ'. There are more than 300 prophecies about him including the virgin birth, the place of his birth, the manner of his death (in great detail) and the place of his burial.

It is possible to read the Bible and miss the whole point. Some of the Jewish people did that. They diligently studied the Scriptures (v. 39) but life was not to be found in the book. The book is the witness that points to Jesus. Life is in Jesus. As someone has put it, 'What is in the old [Testament] concealed is in the new [Testament] revealed.'

In the light of all this evidence, why do people refuse to come to Jesus Christ?

Some are not willing to put God first in their lives (v. 42)
They are not willing to obey the first command (to love God above everything) to give up everything that they know is wrong in their lives.

Some are more concerned about what others think than about what God thinks (v. 44)

There may be a stigma attached to being known as a Christian and associated with other Christians, but Jesus died publicly for us and we should not be ashamed to be known publicly as his followers.

Some simply refuse to believe in Jesus in spite of the evidence (vv. 40, 47)

We should not be surprised if this is still the case today. It is not belief in Jesus that is irrational but unbelief. It is irrational not to believe in the face of overwhelming evidence.

🕊 PRAY

You could thank God that he has not left us without evidence and that our faith is based on good historical grounds. You could thank him for the life, death and resurrection of Jesus Christ.

16   IS CHRISTIANITY A CRUTCH?

LUKE 9:18-27

Jesus Feeds the Five Thousand

[10]When the apostles returned, they reported to Jesus what they had done. Then he took them with him and they withdrew by themselves to a town called Bethsaida, [11]but the crowds learned about it and followed him. He welcomed them and spoke to them about the kingdom of God, and healed those who needed healing.

[12]Late in the afternoon the Twelve came to him and said, "Send the crowd away so they can go to the surrounding villages and countryside and find food and lodging, because we are in a remote place here."

[13]He replied, "You give them something to eat."

They answered, "We have only five loaves of bread and two fish unless we go and buy food for all this crowd." [14](About five thousand men were there.)

But he said to his disciples, "Make them sit down in groups of about fifty each." [15]The disciples did so, and everybody sat down. [16]Taking the five loaves and the two fish and looking up to heaven, he gave thanks and broke them. Then he gave them to the disciples to set before the people. [17]They all ate and were satisfied, and the disciples picked up twelve basketfuls of broken pieces that were left over.

Peter's Confession of Christ

[18]Once when Jesus was praying in private and his disciples were with him, he asked them, "Who do the crowds say I am?"

[19]They replied, "Some say John the Baptist; others say Elijah; and still others, that one of the prophets of long ago has come back to life."

[20]"But what about you?" he asked. "Who do you say I am?"

Peter answered, "The Christ of God."

[21]Jesus strictly warned them not to tell this to anyone. [22]And he said, "The Son of Man must suffer many things and be rejected by the elders, chief priests and teachers of the law, and he must be killed and on the third day be raised to life."

[23]Then he said to them all: "Those who would come after me must deny themselves and take up their cross daily and follow me. [24]For those who want to save their lives will lose them, but those who lose their lives for me will save them. [25]What good is it for you to gain the whole world, and yet lose or forfeit your very self? [26]All who are ashamed of me and my words, the Son of Man will be ashamed of them when he comes in his glory and in the glory of the Father and of the holy angels. [27]I tell you the truth, some who are standing here will not taste death before they see the kingdom of God."

The Transfiguration

[28]About eight days after Jesus said this, he took Peter, John and James with him and went up onto a mountain to pray. [29]As he was praying, the appearance of his face changed, and his clothes became as bright as a flash of lightning. [30]Two men, Moses and Elijah, [31]appeared in glorious splendour, talking with Jesus. They spoke about his departure, which he was about to bring to fulfilment at Jerusalem. [32]Peter and his companions were very sleepy, but when they became fully awake, they saw his glory and

At Buchenwald, a concentration camp, 65,000 people were put
to death by a totalitarian regime that saw the Christian faith as a
threat:

> ... there was one block of cells reserved for prisoners deemed
> especially dangerous or notable. In cell 27 they placed Paul
> Schneider, a Lutheran pastor, who came to be called 'the
> Preacher of Buchenwald' because even from the small window
> in his cell he loudly proclaimed the Gospel of Jesus Christ in
> defiance of the orders of the Gestapo guards. In cell 23 they
> placed Otto Neururer, a Catholic priest, whose work on behalf
> of the Jews and other so-called 'undesirables' had made him a
> threat to the Nazi warlords. He too ministered to the prisoners
> in Jesus' name.

'Toward an Evangelical Ecclesiology' by Timothy George, in Thomas
P. Rausch (ed) *Catholics and Evangelicals*, Paulist Press, 2000, pp. 143–44

Timothy George also wrote,

> *Together, a son of Rome and a son of the Reformation, separated
> no longer by four centuries but only by four cells, walked the way
> of the cross and together bore witness to their Lord.*

Christianity Today, 15 June 1998, p.44

Some people say that Christianity is a
crutch. A crutch is an artificial support,
which is only needed if a part of our body
is not functioning correctly. In general,
people don't need crutches, although
they may make life easier in the short
term. People using crutches are anxious
to get rid of them as soon as possible. Is
Christianity like that?

1. IS CHRISTIANITY AN ARTIFICIAL SUPPORT? (VV. 18–20)

Is it just wishful thinking or is it true? That depends on who Jesus is (vv. 18–20). Jesus asks Peter two questions:

'Who do the crowds say I am?' (v. 18)

They knew he could not be an ordinary man. When he was twelve, people were 'amazed at his understanding and his answers' (Luke 2:47). When they heard his first talk the 'eyes of everyone... were fastened on him' (Luke 4:20). They had seen him heal lepers and those who were paralysed. They had heard his teaching. They had even seen him raise someone from the dead (Luke 7:11–17), and therefore thought he must be the reincarnation of someone great. People are still speculating today about who Jesus might be. But Jesus asks another question.

'Who do you say I am?' (v. 20)

We cannot rely on second-hand opinions. Each one of us has to make our own decision based on the available evidence. Peter's reply is 'The Christ of God.' He was absolutely right. Jesus is the Christ, the Son of God. There is good historical evidence for this in the life, death and resurrection of Jesus Christ. There is good reason to believe. This is not wishful thinking. It is not a crutch. It is not artificial. This is reality.

2. IS IT ONLY FOR ESPECIALLY WEAK OR NEEDY PEOPLE? (VV. 21–23)

Jesus said, 'The Son of Man must suffer.' The Greek word for 'must' means 'necessary for certain great ends'. Jesus came, died and rose again because he loves us. He came 'for certain great ends' – to meet universal needs. We have physical needs such as food, water and air. We can only survive about three months without food, three days without water and three minutes without air. Yet are food, water and air 'crutches'? No, they are universal physical needs.

All human beings, whether they know it or not, have emotional and spiritual needs. We have a need for meaning and purpose, for hope beyond death and for an answer to guilt. The answer to these needs is not a crutch. It is the cross and resurrection of Jesus Christ.

3. IS IT SOMETHING WHICH MAKES LIFE EASIER? (VV. 23–26)
Is Christianity an escape? Is it a quick fix like drugs? Jesus' words make it quite clear that it is not easy, although it is exciting and challenging. It is not easy for three reasons:

No sin
Jesus says that those who follow him must 'deny themselves' (v. 23). We need to give up what we know to be wrong. We cannot hang on to sin. That would be the easy way out.

No self
Jesus says we must take up our cross daily (v. 23). Anyone who had watched a crucifixion would know that this was no easy option. It means a daily dying to our own selfishness.

No secrecy
Jesus calls us to follow him (v. 26). He was asking people to declare their faith in him publicly. We cannot be secret disciples. Jesus wants his followers to stand up and be counted, even when it is difficult to do so. There is no such thing as a private faith. Christianity is not a crutch. It is a cross. Resolve today to follow him.

20

👏 PRAY

Ask for the help of his Holy Spirit to turn your back on everything that you know is wrong, to take up the cross daily and unashamedly to follow Christ. You will be joining with millions of others like Paul Schneider and Otto Neururer who have taken up their crosses and followed Christ and as a result have made an impact on the society around them.

BE PREPARED

LUKE 12:13-21

Warnings and Encouragements

12 Meanwhile, when a crowd of many thousands had gathered, so that they were trampling on one another, Jesus began to speak first to his disciples, saying: "Be on your guard against the yeast of the Pharisees, which is hypocrisy. ²There is nothing concealed that will be disclosed, or hidden that will not be made known. ³What you have said in the dark will be heard in the daylight, and what you have whispered in the ear in the inner rooms will be proclaimed from the roofs.

⁴"I tell you, my friends, do not be afraid of those who kill the body and after that can do no more. ⁵But I will show you whom you should fear: Fear him who, after the killing of the body, has power to throw you into hell. Yes, I tell you, fear him. ⁶Are not five sparrows sold for two pennies? Yet not one of them is forgotten by God. ⁷Indeed, the very hairs of your head are all numbered. Don't be afraid; you are worth more than many sparrows.

⁸"I tell you, those who acknowledge me before others the Son of Man will also acknowledge before the angels of God. ⁹But those who disown me before others will be disowned before the angels of God. ¹⁰And everyone who speaks a word against the Son of Man will be forgiven, but anyone who blasphemes against the Holy Spirit will not be forgiven.

¹¹"When you are brought before synagogues, rulers and authorities, do not worry about how you will defend yourselves or what you will say, ¹²for the Holy Spirit will teach you at that time what you should say."

The Parable of the Rich Fool

¹³Someone in the crowd said to him, "Teacher, tell my brother to divide the inheritance with me."

¹⁴Jesus replied, "Friend, who appointed me a judge or an arbiter between you?" ¹⁵Then he said to them, "Watch out! Be on your guard against all kinds of greed; life does not consist in the abundance of possessions."

¹⁶And he told them this parable: "The ground of a certain rich man produced a good crop. ¹⁷He thought to himself, 'What shall I do? I have no place to store my crops.'

¹⁸"Then he said, 'This is what I'll do. I will tear down my barns and build bigger ones, and there I will store all my grain and my goods. ¹⁹And I'll say to myself, "You have plenty of good things laid up for many years. Take life easy; eat, drink and be merry." '

²⁰"But God said to him, 'You fool! This very night your life will be demanded from you. Then who will get what you have prepared for yourself?'

²¹"This is how it will be with anyone who stores up things for themselves but are not rich towards God."

Do Not Worry

²²Then Jesus said to his disciples: "Therefore I tell you, do not worry about your life, what you will eat; or about your body, what you will wear. ²³Life is more than food, and the body more than clothes. ²⁴Consider the ravens: They do not sow or reap, they have no storeroom or barn; yet God feeds them. And how much more valuable you are than birds! ²⁵Who of you

When Ludwig Nobel died in 1888, a journalist, who mistakenly identified the deceased as Alfred, published his obituary instead. Alfred Bernard Nobel was able to see written before him a summary of the achievements of his life. Materially, it had been a great success – he was very rich. He was a scientific genius; he invented dynamite together with the even more potent solution, blasting gelatin, and in 1880 he patented an almost smokeless gunpowder that European armies rushed to buy. In his obituary he was described as 'the merchant of death'. Alfred Nobel was shocked. Was this all his life had been about? Enabling humankind to destroy itself more efficiently?

This chilling incident caused Nobel to work for world peace. He also rewrote his will. He instructed his executors to convert all his remaining property to cash (it came to $9 million) and to invest it in safe securities, the interest from which would be awarded annually in five prizes to those persons who had contributed most to the benefit of humankind during the preceding year. The five categories were physics, chemistry, medicine, literature and peace. Alfred Nobel died on 10 November 1896. Since then over 600 Nobel Laureates have been recognised.

If you died today what would your obituary say?

Here Jesus tells a story about another 'successful' man – a businessman who had made a lot of money, was considering plans for expanding his company and was looking forward to the prospect of early retirement. Jesus' hearers would have been basking in this tale of wealth and success but Jesus tells us that his obituary was written by God. It was very short – just 'You fool!' The Greek word for 'fool' literally means someone 'without thought'. Although he planned, he did not think about the really important questions of life. Here are three aspects of life which he failed to consider.

1. HE DID NOT THINK ABOUT HIS LONG-TERM FUTURE

This man made two mistakes about the length of his life. First, he assumed he had 'many years' to live (v. 19).

In fact he was to die 'this very night'(v. 20) – and would be required to give an account of his life.

Yet he had never thought beyond this life. In counting on time here, he forgot about eternity. So many people take such a short-term view. A wise person takes a long-term view.

2. HE DID NOT THINK ABOUT THE MEANING OF LIFE

He thought that life was all about having the hallmarks of success: treasure, leisure and pleasure (v. 19).

Treasure

Jesus points out: 'Life does not consist in the abundance of possessions' (v. 15). Material prosperity does not satisfy and anyway it does not last (v. 20).

Leisure

He had planned to 'take life easy'. Leisure is a blessing but it does not give meaning to life.

Pleasure

He was going to 'eat, drink and be merry'. Again, combination never truly satisfies. Life is all about a with God through Jesus Christ and our relationships w

There is nothing wrong with material possessions, play of golf or enjoying our food and drink, but these are not what really about – and all of them make absurd ultimate goals.

3. HE DID NOT THINK ABOUT HIS GREATEST NEED

The words 'I', 'my' and 'myself' appear seven times in verses 17–19. The fool thought he was self-sufficient. He thought he could do it by himself: he didn't need God or anyone else. Actually, he was very self-centred. Self-centredness is the root of the human problem. This is why Jesus came to set us free from the cell of our own self-centredness.

It is worth asking ourselves these questions:

- Do we assume that we have 'many years' or are we ready to meet God today?

- What is our perspective? Is it this life or eternity?

- What are our priorities? Are they treasure, leisure and pleasure or our relationship with God and loving others?

- What is our greatest problem? Do we see our own selfishness and need for forgiveness?

🖐 PRAY

Lord, save me from becoming self-centred. Help me to keep my focus on serving you.

this well-tried
relationship
...th others.
...ing a lot
...fe is

BE PREPARED

25

place, so that when your host comes,

...ed his servant, 'Go out quickly into
...reets and alleys of the town and
...in the poor, the crippled, the blind
...e lame.'
..." 'Sir,' the servant said, 'what you
...ed has been done, but there is still
...
..."Then the master told his servant,
...t to the roads and country lanes
...ake them come in, so that my house
will be full. ²⁴I tell you, not one of those
who were invited will get a taste of my
banquet.'"

invite you back and so you will be repaid.
¹³But when you give a banquet, invite the
poor, the crippled, the lame, the blind,
¹⁴and you will be blessed. Although they
cannot repay you, you will be repaid at the
resurrection of the righteous."

The Parable of the Great Banquet

¹⁵When one of those at the table with
him heard this, he said to Jesus, "Blessed
is the one who will eat at the feast in the
kingdom of God."

¹⁶Jesus replied: "A certain man was
preparing a great banquet and invited
many guests. ¹⁷At the time of the banquet
he sent his servant to tell those who had
been invited, 'Come, for everything is now
ready.'

¹⁸"But they all alike began to make
excuses. The first said, 'I have just bought
a field, and I must go and see it. Please
excuse me.'

¹⁹"Another said, 'I have just bought
five yoke of oxen, and I'm on my way to try
them out. Please excuse me.'

²⁰"Still another said, 'I have just got
married, so I can't come.'

²¹"The servant came back and
reported this to his master. Then the
owner of the house became angry and

The Cost of Being a Disciple

²⁵Large crowds were travelling with
Jesus, and turning to them he said: ²⁶"If
anyone comes to me and does not hate
father and mother, wife and children,
brothers and sisters—yes, even life
itself—such a person cannot be my
disciple. ²⁷And those who do not carry
their cross and follow me cannot be my
disciples.

²⁸"Suppose one of you wants to build
a tower. Will you not first sit down and
estimate the cost to see if you have enough
money to complete it? ²⁹For if you lay the
foundation and are not able to finish it,
everyone who sees it will ridicule you,
³⁰saying, 'This person began to build and
was not able to finish.'

³¹"Or suppose a king is about to go to
war against another king. Will he not first
sit down and consider whether he is able
with ten thousand men to oppose the one
coming against him with twenty thousand?
³²If he is not able, he will send a delegation
while the other is still a long way off and
will ask for terms of peace. ³³In the same

Imagine receiving an invitation to dinner from a prime minister or a monarch. Supposing we were to reply, 'So sorry, I can't make it – I have moved into a new office and I want to go and have a look at it.' Or, 'So sorry, I have bought a new car and I want to try it out.' Or, 'So sorry, we have recently celebrated our first wedding anniversary – so we can't come.' What a missed opportunity! The excuses in verses 18–20 are just like that, irrational and absurd. That is the point. There are different arguments but similar intentions. There is no urgency to look at the field (v. 18) or try out the oxen (v. 19), and this man could have brought any number of his friends and relations (v. 20).

1. WHAT IS THE BANQUET?

Jesus is saying that the Christian life (life in the kingdom of God) is like a banquet. He himself is the host and we experience the lavish hospitality and love of God through him. The other guests are fellow members of the kingdom. So here we experience not only God's love but the love of other Christians as well. We find meaning and purpose in knowing God. We find life beyond death. Our hunger for forgiveness is satisfied. The Holy Spirit provides the only truly satisfying spiritual drink (John 7:37).

2. WHY SHOULD ANYONE NOT WANT TO BE AT THIS PARTY?

In the story Jesus told, all the guests say they are 'too busy'. For some it is their work, for others their possessions and for still others it is relationships. Today, people make equally absurd excuses.

'I have no need of God'

When people say this, they usually mean that they are quite happy without God. What they fail to realise is that our greatest need is not happiness but forgiveness. It takes a very proud person to say that they have no need of forgiveness.

Either we accept what Jesus has done for us on the cross, or else one day we will pay the just penalty ourselves for the things we have done wrong.

'There is too much to give up'

Sometimes, God puts his finger on an area of our lives which we know is wrong and we realise that we would have to give things up in order to enjoy this relationship with God through Jesus.

But we need to remember:

a. God loves us. He asks us only to give up things which do us harm. If I saw some small children playing with a carving knife I would tell them to stop, not to ruin their fun but to stop them getting hurt.

b. What we give up is nothing compared to what we receive. The cost of not becoming a Christian is far greater than the cost of becoming a Christian.

c. What we give up is nothing compared to what Jesus gave up for us when he died on the cross for us.

'There must be a trap'

Sometimes people find it hard to accept that there is anything free in this life. They think it all sounds too easy; there must be some hidden trap. However, what they fail to realise is that although it is free for us, it was not free for Jesus. He paid for it with his own blood. It may be easy for us. But it was not easy for him.

'I'm not good enough'

Not one of us is good enough. Nor can we ever make ourselves good enough for God. But that is why Jesus came.

He made it possible for God to accept us just as we are, whatever we have done and however much of a mess we have made of our lives.

'I could never keep it up'

We are right to think we could never keep it up – we cannot by ourselves. But the Spirit of God, who comes to live within us, gives us the power and the strength to keep going as Christians.

'I'll do it later'

This is perhaps the most common excuse. Sometimes people say, 'I know it's true – but I am not ready.' They put it off. The longer we put it off the harder it becomes and the more we miss out. We never know whether we will get another opportunity. Speaking for myself, my only regret is that I did not accept the gift earlier.

3. HOW DO WE GET TO THE BANQUET?

There is both an invitation – 'Come, for everything is now ready' – (v. 17) and a command – 'Make them come in' (v. 23). It is the love of Christ that draws us to himself (2 Corinthians 5:14). What do we have to do to accept the invitation?

Change our minds
This is the meaning of the word repentance. If we have not accepted the invitation before, we need to say, 'I am sorry. I have made a mistake. I have changed my mind and I want to come.'

Accept
Thank Jesus that he has made abundant and eternal life possible through the cross, and put your trust in him.

Come and receive
Come to the banquet. Come and meet the host, Jesus Christ.
    Come and eat and drink. Be filled with the Holy Spirit.

✋ PRAY

If you have not yet come to the banquet and want to, here is a prayer you could pray.

Lord Jesus Christ,
I am sorry for the things I have done wrong in my life (take a few moments to ask his forgiveness for anything particular that is on your conscience). Please forgive me. I now turn from everything which I know is wrong.

Thank you that you died on the cross for me so that I could be forgiven and set free.

Thank you that you offer me forgiveness and the gift of your Spirit. I now receive that gift.

Please come into my life by your Holy Spirit to be with me forever.

Thank you, Lord Jesus. Amen.

THE DRAMA OF LIFE

LUKE 15:11–32

The Parable of the Lost Coin

⁸"Or suppose a woman has ten silver coins and loses one. Does she not light a lamp, sweep the house and search carefully until she finds it? ⁹And when she finds it, she calls her friends and neighbours together and says, 'Rejoice with me; I have found my lost coin.' ¹⁰In the same way, I tell you, there is rejoicing in the presence of the angels of God over one sinner who repents."

The Parable of the Lost Son

¹¹Jesus continued: "There was a man who had two sons. ¹²The younger one said to his father, 'Father, give me my share of the estate.' So he divided his property between them.

¹³"Not long after that, the younger son got together all he had, set off for a distant country and there squandered his wealth in wild living. ¹⁴After he had spent everything, there was a severe famine in that whole country, and he began to be in need. ¹⁵So he went and hired himself out to a citizen of that country, who sent him to his fields to feed pigs. ¹⁶He longed to fill his stomach with the pods that the pigs were eating, but no-one gave him anything.

¹⁷"When he came to his senses, he said, 'How many of my father's hired servants have food to spare, and here I am starving to death! ¹⁸I will set out and go back to my father and say to him: Father, I have sinned against heaven and against you. ¹⁹I am no longer worthy to be called your son; make me like one of your hired servants.' ²⁰So he got up and went to his father.

"But while he was still a long way off, his father saw him and was filled with compassion for him; he ran to his son, threw his arms around him and kissed him.

²¹"The son said to him, 'Father, I have sinned against heaven and against you. I am no longer worthy to be called your son.'

²²"But the father said to his servants, 'Quick! Bring the best robe and put it on him. Put a ring on his finger and sandals on his feet. ²³Bring the fattened calf and kill it. Let's have a feast and celebrate. ²⁴For this son of mine was dead and is alive again; he was lost and is found.' So they began to celebrate.

²⁵"Meanwhile, the older son was in the field. When he came near the house, he heard music and dancing. ²⁶So he called one of the servants and asked him what was going on. ²⁷'Your brother has come,' he replied, 'and your father has killed the fattened calf because he has him back safe and sound.'

²⁸"The older brother became angry and refused to go in. So his father went out and pleaded with him. ²⁹But he answered his father, 'Look! All these years I've been slaving for you and never disobeyed your orders. Yet you never gave me even a young goat so I could celebrate with my friends. ³⁰But when this son of yours who has squandered your property with prostitutes comes home, you kill the fattened calf for him!'

³¹"'My son,' the father said, 'you are always with me, and everything I have is yours. ³²But we had to celebrate and be glad, because this brother of yours was dead and is alive again; he was lost and is found.' "

This has been called 'the greatest short story ever told'. Jesus chose to tell it to a group of people who had yet to make up their minds about God. In the story the father represents God and the two sons represent you and me. It applies to those who have drifted away from God as well as to those who have never known such a relationship. We can think of it as the drama of life in three acts.

ACT I – THE SEARCH FOR FULFILMENT (VV. 11-12)
SCENE I – THE 'GIVE ME' MENTALITY (V. 12)

The younger son asks to see his father. He already has a share of the estate (v. 12). He has the use of the income. He will receive the capital on his father's death, but he says, 'I want the capital now.' He is saying in effect: 'I don't want anyone else telling me what to do' and so he breaks the relationship with his father. Christianity is about a relationship with God. When we say, 'I can lead my life without God. I don't need you. I don't want you', we break that relationship. The father lets his son go just as God lets us go.

34

SCENE II - FLEETING PLEASURES (V. 13)

He collects 'all he had' (v. 13). Life can never have seemed better. He sees the potential and the opportunities and with a tremor of excitement, he sets off for the Las Vegas of the ancient world with its night clubs, brothels and gambling dens. He leads a 'wild' life (v. 13), but his pleasure is very temporary. He is wasting his life as he 'squandered his wealth' (v. 13).

SCENE III - LIFE WITHOUT GOD (VV. 14-16)

Sense of emptiness

He has 'spent everything' (v. 14). He begins to 'be in need' (v. 14).

Loss of freedom

He looked for freedom but has found slavery (v. 15). He has ended up feeding pigs - an occupation forbidden to the Jews since pigs were regarded as 'unclean'.

Hunger

He longs to fill his stomach with the pods that the pigs eat (v. 16). This is a picture of the hunger deep in our hearts, which can only be satisfied by a relationship with God.

Loneliness

When he had money, he had friends and was surrounded by people. But they deserted him when he was broke. They didn't really care about him as a true friend. When he had money to spend he was all right, but now no one gave him anything (v. 16b).

ACT II - IN THE VALLEY OF DECISION (VV. 17-20A)

He starts to do some thinking

'He came to his senses' (v. 17). He uses his mind. Christianity is not an irrational leap of faith. It is the most rational thing that we can do. Running away from the facts is irrational. It is escapism.

He doesn't worry about his motives

He wants food (v. 17). We will never get our motives right. What matters is doing the right thing.

He plans to turn right round

It is very hard to admit that we are wrong – we all fear losing face. When he left he said, 'Give me.' Now he says, 'Forgive me' (vv. 18-19).

He does something

'He got up and went to his father' (v. 20). Faith involves a decision. It is an act of the will based on what we know.

ACT III – COMING HOME (VV. 20B-24)

The son has forgotten about his father but the father has not forgotten about his son (v. 20b). Every day he watches, waits and hopes. When he sees him he is 'filled with compassion ' (v. 20b). It breaks his heart to see the mess his son has made of his life. He runs (v. 20b). For an elderly oriental man it was not considered dignified to run, but he is not worried about his dignity. He throws his arms around him and kisses him many times.

The son starts his confession (v. 21). The father interrupts. There is no rebuke or reproach, no 'I told you so', no conditions. He says, 'Quick!' (v. 22). He gives him the best robe reserved for the honoured guests and a ring, a sign of confidence and distinction. He gives him shoes. Slaves and even guests did not wear shoes, only the master and his sons. They are a sign of forgiveness and reinstatement. He kills the 'fattened calf'. He throws a party, a feast, a celebration with music and dancing (v. 25). This is a picture of the Christian life.

The older brother is angry (v. 28). He has always been around the home but never really seems to have enjoyed his relationship. He can't understand what all the fuss is about and thinks it is all excessive but he is invited to the party as well. He too could enjoy

36

the benefits of total forgiveness, restored relationships, solid joy and fullness of life.

Don't miss out on the party. Whether you feel more like the younger or the older brother, the key is to get back into a right relationship with the Father and join in the celebrations. If you are not in this relationship you can come home today. Don't worry about your motives.

🖑 PRAY

Pray the prayer the younger son planned to pray (v. 19). Turn to God as your Father and start to enjoy his great love and generosity towards you.

MID-LIFE CRISES

LUKE 19:1–10

Jesus Again Predicts His Death

³¹Jesus took the Twelve aside and told them, "We are going up to Jerusalem, and everything that is written by the prophets about the Son of Man will be fulfilled. ³²He will be turned over to the Gentiles. They will mock him, insult him, spit on him, flog him and kill him. ³³On the third day he will rise again."

³⁴The disciples did not understand any of this. Its meaning was hidden from them, and they did not know what he was talking about.

A Blind Beggar Receives His Sight

³⁵As Jesus approached Jericho, a blind man was sitting by the roadside begging. ³⁶When he heard the crowds going by, he asked what was happening. ³⁷They told him, "Jesus of Nazareth is passing by."

³⁸He called out, "Jesus, Son of David, have mercy on me!"

³⁹Those who led the way rebuked him and told him to be quiet, but he shouted all the more, "Son of David, have mercy on me!"

⁴⁰Jesus stopped and ordered the man to be brought to him. When he came near, Jesus asked him, ⁴¹"What do you want me to do for you?"

"Lord, I want to see," he replied.

⁴²Jesus said to him, "Receive your sight; your faith has healed you." ⁴³Immediately he received his sight and followed Jesus, praising God. When all the people saw it, they also praised God.

Zacchaeus the Tax Collector

19 Jesus entered Jericho and was passing through. ²A man was there by the name of Zacchaeus; he was a chief tax collector and was wealthy. ³He wanted to see who Jesus was, but being a short man he could not, because of the crowd. ⁴So he ran ahead and climbed a sycamore-fig tree to see him, since Jesus was coming that way.

⁵When Jesus reached the spot, he looked up and said to him, "Zacchaeus, come down immediately. I must stay at your house today." ⁶So he came down at once and welcomed him gladly.

⁷All the people saw this and began to mutter, "He has gone to be the guest of a 'sinner'."

⁸But Zacchaeus stood up and said to the Lord, "Look, Lord! Here and now I give half of my possessions to the poor, and if I have cheated anybody out of anything, I will pay back four times the amount."

⁹Jesus said to him, "Today salvation has come to this house, because this man, too, is a son of Abraham. ¹⁰For the Son of Man came to seek and to save what was lost."

The Parable of the Ten Minas

¹¹While they were listening to this, he went on to tell them a parable, because he was near Jerusalem and the people thought that the kingdom of God was going to appear at once. ¹²He said: "A man of noble birth went to a distant country to have himself appointed king and then to return. ¹³So he called ten of his servants and gave them ten minas. 'Put this money to work,' he said, 'until I come back.'

Zacchaeus was probably in mid-life. He was old enough to be at the top of his profession (v. 2), but young enough to climb a tree (v. 4). He was a wealthy man. He had the status of being a chief tax collector with people working under him and had no doubt been promoted many times. He had success but at a cost.

Tax collectors had an appalling reputation for corruption and collaborating with the occupying Roman power. He had worked hard for the sake of his family but they must have faced ostracism owing to his line of work and unpopularity.

His parents had called him Zacchaeus meaning 'the righteous one' – but now perhaps he had no time for God. Religious people regarded him as a 'sinner' (v. 7). In the light of all this, perhaps he was facing a mid-life crisis!

1. WHY DID HE WANT TO SEE JESUS? (VV. 3-4)
Two things he realised:

First, he realised he had a need. Despite all his money and success there was still something missing.

Second, he realised that Jesus might provide the key. 'He wanted to see who Jesus was' (v. 3). The most important question we can ever ask is, 'Who is Jesus?'

Four things he did not realise:
First, he did not realise that you cannot hide from Jesus. He
wanted to see Jesus without Jesus seeing him (v. 4) – he probably
felt guilty. But none of us can hide. Jesus knew him.

He knew his name. For a Hebrew, if someone knew your name,
they knew a great deal about you. God knows all about us.

Second, he did not realise that Jesus loved him in spite of his
sin (Romans 5:8). Jesus picked him out in a crowd. Jesus sees us
wherever we are. He was on his way to Jerusalem to die on a cross
for us all. He was going to die for Zacchaeus (Galatians 2:20).

Third, he did not realise that Jesus wanted to know him (v. 5).
This is the heart of the Christian faith: knowing Jesus Christ.

Fourth, he did not realise that Jesus required a response
(v. 5). This is a moment of high drama. Jesus says, 'Come down
immediately.' How was Zacchaeus to respond?

2. HOW DID ZACCHAEUS RESPOND? (VV. 6–7)
First, he 'came down'. He obeyed Jesus and humbled himself.
Second, he did not put it off. He came down 'at once'. Third, he
'welcomed him'. Fourth, he did so 'gladly'. At last he had found
happiness – but in an unexpected way. Fifth, he was not put off by
the crowd's attitude (v. 7). They were shocked and said in effect,
'He is not the religious type.' But Zacchaeus didn't care what the
people thought.

3. WHAT HAPPENED AS A RESULT? (VV. 8, 10)
A total transformation took place in Zacchaeus' attitude, his life,
his friends and in the society around him.

His attitude
He completely changed his attitude to his possessions. His
experience of Jesus put everything else in perspective. It was no
longer, 'How much can I get?' but rather, 'How much can I give?'

(v. 8). He started to get his life sorted out by paying back what he owed. It was his relationship with Jesus Christ that enabled him to do this.

His life
Zacchaeus had found forgiveness and a totally new start (v. 9). The mess of the past had been cleared up. He had found freedom from the rat race. He had discovered that his future was secure through a relationship with Christ which was to go on forever.

His family
Jesus said, 'Today salvation has come to this house' (v. 9). Everyone in the household was included.

Society
The poor benefited. He gave half his possessions to the poor (v. 8). Justice was done: those who had been cheated were repaid.

We don't have to go through a mid-life crisis to receive Jesus. He says to each of us that he wants to stay at our house today. If you have not yet done so why not invite him in today? Ask him to show you how much he loves you. Think about the fact that he died for you. Ask him to show you if there is anything you need to put right in your life. If there is, why not follow Zacchaeus' example and do so right away?

🖐 PRAY

You might like to pray the famous prayer that an African girl prayed.

'O great Chief, light a candle within my heart that I may see what is there and sweep the rubbish from your dwelling place.'

WHAT IS THE GOSPEL?

1 CORINTHIANS 15:1-11

[27]Two or three prophets should speak, and the others should weigh carefully what is said. [30]And if a revelation comes to someone who is sitting down, the first speaker should stop. [31]For you can all prophesy in turn so that everyone may be instructed and encouraged. [32]The spirits of prophets are subject to the control of prophets. [33]For God is not a God of disorder but of peace.

As in all the congregations of the saints, [34]women should remain silent in the churches. They are not allowed to speak, but must be in submission, as the Law says. [35]If they want to enquire about something, they should ask their own husbands at home; for it is disgraceful for a woman to speak in the church.

[36]Did the word of God originate with you? Or are you the only people it has reached? [37]If any think they are prophets or are spiritually gifted, let them acknowledge that what I am writing to you is the Lord's command. [38]Those who ignore this will themselves be ignored.

[39]Therefore, my brothers and sisters, be eager to prophesy, and do not forbid speaking in tongues. [40]But everything should be done in a fitting and orderly way.

The Resurrection of Christ

15 Now, brothers and sisters, I want to remind you of the gospel I preached to you, which you received and on which you have taken your stand. [2]By this gospel you are saved, if you hold firmly to the word I preached to you. Otherwise, you have believed in vain.

[3]For what I received I passed on to you as of first importance: that Christ died for our sins according to the Scriptures, [4]that he was buried, that he was raised on the third day according to the Scriptures, [5]and that he appeared to Peter, and then to the Twelve. [6]After that, he appeared to more than five hundred of the brothers and sisters at the same time, most of whom are still living, though some have fallen asleep. [7]Then he appeared to James, then to all the apostles, [8]and last of all he appeared to me also, as to one abnormally born.

[9]For I am the least of the apostles and do not even deserve to be called an apostle, because I persecuted the church of God. [10]But by the grace of God I am what I am, and his grace to me was not without effect. No, I worked harder than all of them—yet not I, but the grace of God that was with me. [11]Whether, then, it was I or they, this is what we preach, and this is what you believed.

The Resurrection of the Dead

[12]But if it is preached that Christ has been raised from the dead, how can some of you say that there is no resurrection of the dead? [13]If there is no resurrection of the dead, then not even Christ has been raised. [14]And if Christ has not been raised, our preaching is useless and so is your faith. [15]More than that, we are then found to be false witnesses about God, for we have testified about God that he raised Christ from the dead. But he did not raise him if in fact the dead are not raised. [16]For if the dead are not raised, then Christ has not been raised either. [17]And if Christ has not been raised, your faith is futile; you are still in your sins. [18]Then those also who

What was the church saying about Jesus three years after he died? The book of Corinthians is an early Christian document. It was written about AD 54 (around twenty years after the events described). However, Paul here appears to be referring to an even earlier record. He speaks of having 'received' and 'passed on' (v. 3) the gospel. These are technical words for receiving and handing on an authorised tradition. We know from elsewhere in the New Testament that he received this tradition within three years of the crucifixion. This may well be the earliest creed of the church. What is its message?

43

> " Isn't it a musical? "

Paul says he wants to remind his readers about the gospel. The gospel means good news. It is a message that brings great joy. It is good news about a person. The Corinthians received this news. They took their stand on it (v. 1) and by it they were 'saved' (v. 2). The modern way of putting that would be to say that they found freedom. What is the message of the gospel?

1. THE DEATH OF CHRIST (VV. 3-4)
The person
The person who died was the 'Christ' (v. 3) – the Messiah, literally the 'anointed one'. He was a fully human being but he was more than just another person. He was the Son of God.

The plan

It was no mistake. He died 'according to the Scriptures' (vv. 3–4). Jesus is unique in the history of humankind as his life and death were both described up to hundreds of years beforehand.

The purpose

His death was 'for our sins' (v. 3). The good news is that Jesus' death on the cross has made possible the forgiveness of our sins. The weight of our guilt has been removed because he has broken the power of sin, freeing us from every addiction. Every enemy has been defeated. He has disarmed the principalities and powers of evil, defeating every possible enemy. We have nothing to fear.

2. THE RESURRECTION OF CHRIST (VV. 4–8)

'He was buried' (v. 4)

Dying and being buried does not distinguish him from others. Mohammed, Alexander the Great, Marx and Abraham Lincoln died and were buried. But...

'He was raised' (v. 4)

This is the earliest historical reference to the empty tomb.

The Greek word for 'raised' refers to something that happened in the past but whose effect remains in force. Having been raised by God, Jesus is alive today. No one else in the history of the world has been 'raised' and is still alive.

'He appeared' (vv. 5–8)

Paul does not give an exhaustive list of the appearances but enough to show they were well-attested. He appeared to Peter (Luke 24:34), to the twelve apostles and to over 500 others, then to all the apostles (more than the twelve), then to James, the brother of Jesus. Finally, he appeared to Paul, who is writing here his own first-hand account (v. 8).

One day Paul was at the stoning of Stephen, hungry for the blood of Christians, approving his death, destroying the church, dragging Christians off to prison and breathing out murderous threats against them. Within a few days he was preaching that Jesus was the Son of God (Acts 7:54 – 9:22).

The resurrection is rooted in history, grounded in Scripture and confirmed by experience.

The great news for us is that the past has been dealt with. Jesus died for our sins, thereby removing our guilt. The resurrection attests to the achievement of the cross.

Second, our future is secure. Death is certain but for the Christian it is only 'falling asleep'. It is not to be feared. We expect to wake up in the morning. In the rest of 1 Corinthians chapter 15, Paul assures his readers that one day they too will have a resurrection body.

Third, the present takes on a new dimension. Jesus is alive. We can know him. This is the heart of Christianity: a relationship with a living person who gives meaning and purpose to life. What are we to do? Paul's answer here is that we should receive this news, believe it, hold firmly to it and pass it on.

Paul received this good news. He passed it on to the Corinthians, they believed it and passed it on. It has since been passed on to us down the centuries. Now it is our turn. We have been entrusted with the message. Our task is to pass it on to our generation in a language that they can understand.

45

🖐 PRAY

This would be a good moment to thank God for the gospel. Thank Jesus for dying for you. Thank him that he is alive and with you. Pray for 'the grace of God' (v.10) to be with you as you pass on the good news to others that they too might find this freedom.

+ + + + + + + +

DAY 9

KNOW WHAT YOU'VE GOT

EPHESIANS 1:15–23

Spiritual Blessings in Christ

3Praise be to the God and Father of our Lord Jesus Christ, who has blessed us in the heavenly realms with every spiritual blessing in Christ. 4For he chose us in him before the creation of the world to be holy and blameless in his sight. In love 5he predestined us to be adopted as his children through Jesus Christ, in accordance with his pleasure and will—6to the praise of his glorious grace, which he has freely given us in the One he loves. 7In him we have redemption through his blood, the forgiveness of sins, in accordance with the riches of God's grace 8that he lavished on us with all wisdom and understanding. 9And he made known to us the mystery of his will according to his good pleasure, which he purposed in Christ, 10to be put into effect when the times will have reached their fulfilment—to bring all things in heaven and on earth together under one head, even Christ.

11In him we were also chosen, having been predestined according to the plan of him who works out everything in conformity with the purpose of his will, 12in order that we, who were the first to hope in Christ, might be for the praise of his glory. 13And you also were included in Christ when you heard the word of truth, the gospel of your salvation. Having believed, you were marked in him with a seal, the promised Holy Spirit, 14who is a deposit guaranteeing our inheritance until the redemption of those who are God's possession—to the praise of his glory.

Thanksgiving and Prayer

15For this reason, ever since I heard about your faith in the Lord Jesus and your love for all the saints, 16I have not stopped giving thanks for you, remembering you in my prayers. 17I keep asking that the God of our Lord Jesus Christ, the glorious Father, may give you the Spirit of wisdom and revelation, so that you may know him better. 18I pray also that the eyes of your heart may be enlightened in order that you may know the hope to which he has called you, the riches of his glorious inheritance in the saints, 19and his incomparably great power for us who believe. That power is like the working of his mighty strength, 20which he exerted in Christ when he raised him from the dead and seated him at his right hand in the heavenly realms, 21far above all rule and authority, power and dominion, and every title that can be given, not only in the present age but also in the one to come. 22And God placed all things under his feet and appointed him to be head over everything for the church, 23which is his body, the fulness of him who fills everything in every way.

Made Alive in Christ

2 As for you, you were dead in your transgressions and sins, 2in which you used to live when you followed the ways of this world and of the ruler of the kingdom of the air, the spirit who is now at work in those who are disobedient. 3All of us also lived among them at one time, gratifying the cravings of our sinful nature and following its desires and thoughts. Like the rest, we were by nature objects of wrath. 4But because of his great love for us, God, who is rich in mercy, 5made us alive with Christ even when we were

William Randolph Hearst (1863–1951), on whose life the film Citizen Kane was based, built up the largest newspaper chain in the United States during the 1920s. He built himself a grandiose castle on a 240,000-acre ranch in California. It contained a vast collection of antiques and objets d'art in which he invested a huge fortune. He collected them from all over the world and stored them in warehouses in different places.

One day he came across the description of a valuable piece of art in a magazine. He was determined to get hold of it, but no one knew where it was. He sent his agent all over the world to find it. Months and months went by. Finally the man came back and reported, 'Mr Hearst, I have found it.' With great joy he asked, 'Where? Where was it?' The man replied, 'It was in your warehouse. You bought it years ago.'

47

" How disappointing; - I wanted the retail therapy. "

William Randolph Hearst had been frantically searching for what he already possessed. Many Christians are frantically searching for what they already possess. Paul prays that we might know what we already possess in Christ.

He prays for the Ephesians that they may know four things that they already possess in Christ.

1. THE MOST EXCITING RELATIONSHIP POSSIBLE (V. 17)

The whole Trinity is involved in this relationship: 'the glorious Father', 'our Lord Jesus Christ' and the 'Spirit of wisdom and revelation' who enables us to know God better. This is the purpose for which we were made. This is what gives meaning to life.

Jesus Christ has risen from the dead. The same Jesus who died on the cross is alive and present with us now, as he will be for ever. Therefore, any person anywhere at any time has the opportunity to enjoy the same kind of relationship with him as the disciples had with him in person about 2,000 years ago.

2. A TOTALLY SECURE FUTURE (V. 18B)

So many people are worried about the future. In Christ our future is entirely secure. Paul prays that we might know 'the hope to which he has called you'.

One young man had recently come to Christ when his mother died. He wrote to me about his experience of the funeral: 'I suddenly understood what it meant to be a Christian. In those thirty minutes my eyes were fully opened for the first time. I realised why I had not been racked with grief and bitterness at the loss of my mother – sure I had cried and I was saddened, but I knew – I know – that her faith in Jesus Christ had saved her, and that she would enjoy eternal life.

'I had seen it in her eyes just before she died last Thursday, and yesterday I felt the realisation flood through me – warm, rich and comforting. It was then that I finally understood the enormity of the sacrifice Jesus made for us on the cross, that we really can have eternal life in heaven, through him.'

3. EXTRAORDINARY RICHES (V. 18B)

Paul prays that we would know 'the riches of his glorious inheritance in the saints' (v. 18). One day we will see God and we will worship him face to face. We will be together with all who have died in faith and we will have perfect fellowship with one another. There will be a great multitude there with us. We will become like Christ both in our bodies and in our characters. The enjoyment of this inheritance begins now as we get a foretaste of the future.

49

4. THE POWER OF GOD IN US (V. 19)

Paul refers to 'his incomparably great power for us who believe'. Power belongs to God but he has come to live in us. As Paul searches for words which will adequately describe this power, he recalls the resurrection and ascension of Jesus.

A public demonstration of the power of God took place in history (v. 20a). It started in a cemetery with a corpse. The dead body of Jesus was raised. Neither death nor hell nor Satan nor sin nor demons could hold him.

He ascended (vv. 20b–21). God 'seated him at his right hand in the heavenly realms, far above all rule and authority, power and dominion'. He was then given 'every title that can be given, not only in the present age but also in the one to come'.

In this context, 'right hand' means the place of highest honour and authority. The queen was reminded of this at her coronation. When the orb was placed in her hand, she was told, 'When you see this orb set under the cross, remember that the whole world is subject to the power and empire of Christ our Redeemer.'

In verse 22a we hear that 'God placed all things under his feet'. This is a symbol of his sovereignty. It is a metaphor derived from the sphere of warfare: sometimes victorious kings would place their feet on the necks of the defeated enemy (eg Joshua 10:24; Isaiah 51:23).

God 'appointed him to be head over everything for the church, which is his body, the fulness of him that fills everything in every way'(vv. 22b–23). Christ is the head of the church and the church is his body. Why is the church described as the 'fulness of him who fills everything in every way'? Because the church completes Christ in the same way as a body completes a head. But the church can only function properly if it is constantly being filled with God's power. God's power is available for us, his church. His plans for a united Christian universe are in the hands of the church.

"my life is hard enough without a vision for other peoples."

How big is our vision? Is it simply for our own life? If it is, is that not a little self-centred? Perhaps it stretches to include our family, our friends, our city, maybe our nation or even the entire world. Paul's vision is for a united Christian universe under the Lordship of Christ. The church is God's instrument for achieving this. We can never rest in this life until that is complete. We cannot rest while there is widespread poverty, appalling third world debt, rising crime rates and so on.

It is no good saying, 'We can't do anything.' Paul prays that we would see the potential we have in Christ. He prays that we would get to know him better and thus start to see our individual and collective calling, our inheritance and the power he has given us to move forward from where we are now to where God would like us to be. Do we see the task that God has entrusted to his church? We cannot rest until the whole universe is subject to his reign – 'the fulness of him who fills everything in every way' (v. 23).

🖐 PRAY

This is a good moment to thank God for everything he has given us, and which we already possess in Christ. We could thank him for our relationship with him, for the hope that he gives us, for his promised inheritance, for the fact that he raised Jesus from the dead and that the same power is available for us now.

RESCUED

EPHESIANS 2:1-10

the gospel of your salvation. Having believed, you were marked in him with a seal, the promised Holy Spirit, ¹⁴who is a deposit guaranteeing our inheritance until the redemption of those who are God's possession—to the praise of his glory.

Thanksgiving and Prayer

¹⁵For this reason, ever since I heard about your faith in the Lord Jesus and your love for all the saints, ¹⁶I have not stopped giving thanks for you, remembering you in my prayers. ¹⁷I keep asking that the God of our Lord Jesus Christ, the glorious Father, may give you the Spirit of wisdom and revelation, so that you may know him better. ¹⁸I pray also that the eyes of your heart may be enlightened in order that you may know the hope to which he has called you, the riches of his glorious inheritance in the saints, ¹⁹and his incomparably great power for us who believe. That power is like the working of his mighty strength, ²⁰which he exerted in Christ when he raised him from the dead and seated him at his right hand in the heavenly realms, ²¹far above all rule and authority, power and dominion, and every title that can be given, not only in the present age but also in the one to come. ²²And God placed all things under his feet and appointed him to be head over everything for the church, ²³which is his body, the fulness of him who fills everything in every way.

Made Alive in Christ

2 As for you, you were dead in your transgressions and sins, ²in which you used to live when you followed the ways of this world and of the ruler of the kingdom of the air, the spirit who is now at work in those who are disobedient. ³All of us also lived among them at one time, gratifying the cravings of our sinful nature and following its desires and thoughts. Like the rest, we were by nature objects of wrath. ⁴But because of his great love for us, God, who is rich in mercy, ⁵made us alive with Christ even when we were dead in transgressions—it is by grace you have been saved. ⁶And God raised us up with Christ and seated us with him in the heavenly realms in Christ Jesus, ⁷in order that in the coming ages he might show the incomparable riches of his grace, expressed in his kindness to us in Christ Jesus. ⁸For it is by grace you have been saved, through faith—and this not from yourselves, it is the gift of God—⁹not by works, so that no-one can boast. ¹⁰For we are God's handiwork, created in Christ Jesus to do good works, which God prepared in advance for us to do.

One in Christ

¹¹Therefore, remember that formerly you who are Gentiles by birth and called "uncircumcised" by those who call themselves "the circumcision" (that done in the body by human hands)— ¹²remember that at that time you were separate from Christ, excluded from citizenship in Israel and foreigners to the covenants of the promise, without hope and without God in the world. ¹³But now in Christ Jesus you who once were far away have been brought near by the blood of Christ.

¹⁴For he himself is our peace, who has made the two groups one and has destroyed the barrier, the dividing wall of

If you go into a jeweller's shop and you want a diamond ring, the jeweller lays a black velvet cloth on the counter. Then the diamond ring is placed right in the middle of that black cloth. Against the black background the diamond sparkles in all its beauty. Similarly, we cannot see the wonder and wealth of God's love until we see it against the backdrop of our sin.

1. WHAT HAVE WE BEEN RESCUED FROM? (VV. 1–3)
Death (v. 1)
We were dead and unresponsive as a corpse. We did not recognise the love of God, the identity of Jesus or the power of the Holy Spirit. We were intended to live in a relationship with God but two things broke that relationship: our trespasses (times when we crossed God's boundaries and did what we knew to be wrong) and our sins (where we fell short and failed to do what we should have done).

Disobedience (vv. 2–3)
When we have no relationship with God we act as everybody else seems to be acting. We follow 'the ways of this world' (v. 2). In this context, 'world' means society organised without reference to God. The devil (v. 2b) controls the lives of those who are disobedient to God, encouraging them to follow the instincts of their sinful nature. It is easy to find oneself enslaved by the world, the flesh and the devil.

Doom (v. 3)
We were 'by nature... objects of wrath'. We have all been found guilty, and guilt requires a sentence. 'Wrath' means righteous anger. It is God's personal, righteous constant hostility to evil. It is the inevitable reaction of a holy God to sin.

The diagnosis is as bad as it possibly could be. This is the condition of every man and woman without Christ. A dead person can do nothing to make themselves alive.

2. HOW HAVE WE BEEN RESCUED? (VV. 4-9)

What has God done?

Two of the greatest words in the Bible are: 'But... God' (v. 4). The rescue came by God's initiative because he loves us so much. It was a result of 'his great love'. From the first page of the Bible to the last the message is that 'God loves you'.

The rescue – the crucifixion of Christ – arose out of God's mercy. He is 'rich in mercy', full of forgiveness and grace.

What can we do?

Paul makes two negative points. First, we cannot save ourselves (v. 8). We cannot contribute to our rescue. Second, it is not 'by works' (v. 9). We cannot do it by our own efforts and achievements.

Then he makes two positive points. First, it is 'by grace' (v. 8). It is God's free and undeserved mercy to us. The children's definition of grace is 'God's Riches At Christ's Expense'. Second, it is 'through faith' (v. 8). It is a gift. We can only say, 'Thank you'. We do not earn it by our faith. Faith is the way in which we receive the gift.

3. WHAT ARE WE RESCUED FOR? (VV. 5-10)

Resurrection (v. 5)

We are no longer dead but 'made alive' (v. 5). We are 'raised up with Christ and seated... in the heavenly realms' (v. 6). Christ's own bodily resurrection points the way to our own.

Future hope (v. 7)

We are no longer facing judgment but have the most exciting future hope, to enjoy God's kindness for all eternity – 'the incomparable riches of his grace, expressed in his kindness to us in Christ Jesus' (v. 7).

Prepared plan (v. 10)

God has prepared in advance 'good works' for us to do. Paul wholeheartedly repudiated good works as grounds for salvation but wholeheartedly insisted on them as the fruit of it.

55

🖐 PRAY

We should continue to thank God for all he has done for us – for his great love, his mercy, and his grace. Thank him for his rescue, his kindness, for the 'riches of his grace' and the plan he has for your future. Pray for his guidance and help as you seek to do the 'good works' he has prepared for you to do.

THIS IS YOUR LIFE

JOHN 4:4–26

Jesus Talks With a Samaritan Woman

4 The Pharisees heard that Jesus was gaining and baptising more disciples than John, ²although in fact it was not Jesus who baptised, but his disciples. ³When the Lord learned of this, he left Judea and went back once more to Galilee.

⁴Now he had to go through Samaria. ⁵So he came to a town in Samaria called Sychar, near the plot of ground Jacob had given to his son Joseph. ⁶Jacob's well was there, and Jesus, tired as he was from the journey, sat down by the well. It was about the sixth hour.

⁷When a Samaritan woman came to draw water, Jesus said to her, "Will you give me a drink?" ⁸(His disciples had gone into the town to buy food.)

⁹The Samaritan woman said to him, "You are a Jew and I am a Samaritan woman. How can you ask me for a drink?"(For Jews do not associate with Samaritans.)

¹⁰Jesus answered her, "If you knew the gift of God and who it is that asks you for a drink, you would have asked him and he would have given you living water."

¹¹"Sir," the woman said, "you have nothing to draw with and the well is deep. Where can you get this living water? ¹²Are you greater than our father Jacob, who gave us the well and drank from it himself, as did also his sons and his flocks and herds?"

¹³Jesus answered, "All who drink this water will be thirsty again, ¹⁴but those who drink the water I give them will never thirst. Indeed, the water I give them will become in them a spring of water welling up to eternal life."

¹⁵The woman said to him, "Sir, give me this water so that I won't get thirsty and have to keep coming here to draw water."

¹⁶He told her, "Go, call your husband and come back."

¹⁷"I have no husband," she replied.

Jesus said to her, "You are right when you say you have no husband. ¹⁸The fact is, you have had five husbands, and the man you now have is not your husband. What you have just said is quite true."

¹⁹"Sir," the woman said, "I can see that you are a prophet. ²⁰Our ancestors worshipped on this mountain, but you Jews claim that the place where we must worship is in Jerusalem."

²¹Jesus declared, "Believe me, woman, a time is coming when you will worship the Father neither on this mountain nor in Jerusalem. ²²You Samaritans worship what you do not know; we worship what we do know, for salvation is from the Jews. ²³Yet a time is coming and has now come when the true worshippers will worship the Father in spirit and truth, for they are the kind of worshippers the Father seeks. ²⁴God is spirit, and his worshippers must worship in spirit and in truth."

²⁵The woman said, "I know that Messiah" (called Christ) "is coming. When he comes, he will explain everything to us."

²⁶Then Jesus declared, "I who speak to you am he."

The Disciples Rejoin Jesus

²⁷Just then his disciples returned and were surprised to find him talking with a woman. But no-one asked, "What do

In the long-running television programme *This is Your Life* a person's life was revealed by the presenter Michael Aspel. In this account (and without the help of a team of researchers!) a woman's life is revealed by Jesus Christ. This is one of the most amazing conversations that has ever taken place and it sends the woman rushing back to her town saying to people, 'Come, see a man who told me everything I ever did' (v. 29).

1. WHO IS THIS?

Some say Jesus is just a good religious teacher. But Jesus claims to be far more than that. When the conversation turns to the subject of the Messiah, Jesus categorically declares: 'I who speak to you am he' (v. 26). When he starts to speak metaphorically of living water, he is claiming to be the one who can answer her deepest needs (vv. 10, 13–14). John later explains that this water is the Holy Spirit 'whom those who believed in him were later to receive' (John 7:39).

Others see Jesus as some distant God – but this passage emphasises his humanity. He could be hot, tired, thirsty and hungry. He is certainly not remote. He understands how hard life can be. While living on earth he knew what it was like to have no money, to be hungry, to live without a roof over his head, to be in physical pain, tortured and rejected by his friends. This is the person who was able to help the Samaritan woman, and is able to help us today.

2. WHAT IS HE LIKE?

Jesus is the most loving person who has ever lived. In this passage we see the warmth of his love. He broke all the conventions of his time. First, he broke the rabbinic rules by speaking to a woman in public. Second, he broke the barriers of race (v. 9). The Samaritans were regarded as half-castes and hated. People would walk seventy miles out of their way to avoid contact with them. Although she was a Samaritan Jesus spoke to her. Third, he broke the barriers of lifestyle. Jesus was, among other things, a Jewish religious teacher. She was a sexually promiscuous woman. The religious did not mix with sinners. But the love of Jesus Christ broke down every barrier.

3. WHAT DOES HE OFFER?

Well-water percolates and then gathers in a stagnant pool. In contrast, Jesus offers 'a spring of water' (v. 14), meaning bubbling running water. He contrasts well-water and spring water. He also contrasts the physical with the spiritual. This (spiritual) water wells up to eternal life (v. 14). So he also contrasts the short- and long-term. We drink physical water knowing that we will be thirsty again, but this is living, loving, lasting water. Nothing else can satisfy us into eternity. We can appear to be satisfied by materialism, pleasure or status, but none of them truly satisfies.

There is more to life than money, possessions, work, sport, fame and even human relationships. The woman had tried to gain fulfilment through human relationships, and they did not satisfy. Only a relationship with God through Jesus Christ with the Spirit of God living within us can provide us with the water that satisfies.

4. HOW DID SHE REACT?

Her life is a mess underneath the surface (like most of our lives) – see vv. 16–18. She reacts in an extraordinary way. She attempts to divert his attention away from her and starts talking about mountains (vv. 19–20).

Perhaps she did not want to face up to the reality of her life: the broken relationships, emptiness and guilt.

" In summer you can climb the west face, and even take a picnic. Um, its made of granite, and is dark grey...

Perhaps she felt she had fallen too far. But Jesus came to die for all of us, whatever we have done, and his death on a cross makes forgiveness for everyone possible.

5. WHAT DOES JESUS DO?

Through Jesus her life is transformed. She receives forgiveness for the past. She receives new life in the present and new life for the future – eternal life. Through an ordinary encounter Jesus changed many people's lives forever. He still loves to do this today by giving people the 'gift of God' (v. 10): a new and satisfying life which lasts.

59

 # PRAY

We can receive this gift too. If you would like to, speak to Jesus saying sorry for your past lived without him, thanking him for the gift of new life and asking him to give you now the living water.

Ask him to fill you to overflowing. He promises that if we ask him, God will give us this 'living water' (v.10). This water will become in you 'a spring of water welling up to eternal life' (v.14).

TRUE FREEDOM

JOHN 8:31-36

you will die in your sin. Where I go, you cannot come."

²²This made the Jews ask, "Will he kill himself? Is that why he says, 'Where I go, you cannot come'?"

²³But he continued, "You are from below; I am from above. You are of this world; I am not of this world. ²⁴I told you that you would die in your sins; if you do not belief that I am the one I claim to be, you will indeed die in your sins."

²⁵"Who are you?" they asked. "Just what I have been claiming all along," Jesus replied. ²⁶"I have much to say in judgment of you. But he who sent me is reliable, and what I have heard from him I tell the world."

²⁷They did not understand that he was telling them about his Father. ²⁸So Jesus said, "When you have lifted up the Son of Man, then you will know that I am the one I claim to be and that I do nothing on my own but speak just what the Father has taught me. ²⁹The one who sent me is with me; he has not left me alone, for I always do what pleases him." ³⁰Even as he spoke, many put their faith in him.

The Children of Abraham

³¹To the Jews who had believed him, Jesus said, "If you hold to my teaching, you are really my disciples. ³²Then you will know the truth, and the truth will set you free."

³³They answered him, "We are Abraham's descendants and have never been slaves of anyone. How can you say that we shall be set free?"

³⁴Jesus replied, "I tell you the truth, everyone who sins is a slave to sin. ³⁵Now a slave has no permanent place in the family, but a son belongs to it for ever. ³⁶So if the Son sets you free, you will be free indeed. ³⁷I know you are Abraham's descendants. Yet you are ready to kill me, because you have no room for my word. ³⁸I am telling you what I have seen in the Father's presence, and you do what you have heard from your father."

³⁹"Abraham is our father," they answered.

"If you were Abraham's children," said Jesus, "then you would do the things Abraham did. ⁴⁰As it is, you are determined to kill me, a man who has told you the truth that I heard from God. Abraham did not do such things. ⁴¹You are doing the things your own father does."

"We are not illegitimate children they protested. "The only Father we have is God himself."

The Children of the Devil

⁴²Jesus said to them, "If God were your Father, you would love me, for I came from God and now am here. I have not come on my own; but he sent me. ⁴³Why is my language not clear to you? Because you are unable to hear what I say. ⁴⁴You belong to your father, the devil, and you want to carry out your father's desire. He was a murderer from the beginning, not holding to the truth, for there is no truth in him. When he lies, he speaks his native language, for he is a liar and the father of lies. ⁴⁵Yet because I tell the truth, you do not believe me! ⁴⁶Can any of you prove me guilty of sin? If I am telling the truth, why don't you believe me? ⁴⁷He who belongs to God hears what God says. The reason you do not hear is that

There are many different forms of freedom. There is national freedom: a country is free from being governed by another country. There is political freedom, including free speech, worship, elections, movement and a free press. There is racial freedom, the freedom from racial discrimination, as witnessed in the struggle against apartheid in South Africa. There is individual freedom which is lost, for example, when people are taken hostage. All these are great freedoms, worth fighting for and in some cases worth dying for.

61

But there is an even greater freedom, one worth giving everything for. The freedom which Jesus speaks of here is the highest and purest form and it is independent and different from all the others. On the one hand you can have none of the freedoms listed above and still be free. In the last 2,000 years men and women have willingly given up all these 'outward' freedoms because they wanted to attain something better. On the other hand you can have all the other freedoms and still not be free. The freedom Jesus offers is a personal and inner freedom of the soul. It is vital for us all. What does it mean?

1. FREEDOM OF THE HEART (V. 36)

Jesus points out that sin leads to slavery (v. 34). Sin is self-centred. It involves self-assertion, pride and arrogance. It can involve selfish ambition: the lust for power, money and glory. It sometimes leads to selfish indulgence including drugs, alcoholism or sexual immorality. All this makes us 'a slave to sin'.

But Jesus promises that 'if the Son sets you free, you will be free indeed' (v. 36).

Freedom from guilt

Guilt destroys. The only place to get rid of guilt is at the cross.

Freedom from addictive power

Addiction destroys but Jesus sets us free. We are not necessarily set free from temptation, but we are free from the addictive power of sin.

Freedom from death

The wages of sin is death (Romans 6:23). Jesus sets us free to look death in the face (Hebrews 2:14–15). He gives us eternal life (John 17:3).

Charles Kingsley said that there are two freedoms. First, there is false freedom, where a person is free to do what they like. Second, there is true freedom, where a person is free to do what they ought. Jesus sets us free to be our true selves as God intended us to be. He sets us free to love God, to love our neighbour as ourselves and even to love ourselves in the sense of accepting ourselves as we are.

2. FREEDOM OF THE MIND (V. 32)

Christians are sometimes accused of being 'narrow-minded' or 'anti-intellectual' – as contrasted with 'free thinking'. Jesus says here that the opposite is true. Following Jesus is the way of intellectual freedom and integrity. The 'truth' (v. 32) is what has been revealed by God. Jesus is the truth (John14:6), God's ultimate revelation. Knowing 'the truth' is not about assenting to philosophical principles but about knowing a person. Knowing God and Jesus broadens our minds, gives us depth of insight and scope of understanding. It does not provide all the answers, but gives us a true and reliable framework of thinking, a firm basis which allows us to explore life in all its fullness.

There is no greater freedom than the one Jesus offers. So let us fight for all the freedoms but let us first make sure that we have the freedom that Jesus alone gives.

Read again v. 32: 'Then you will know the truth, and the truth will set you free.' This is a great verse to learn by heart. We find freedom in knowing Jesus Christ: developing a relationship with God through prayer, reading the Bible, obeying him and serving him. It is as we submit completely to God that we encounter true freedom.

63

🖐 PRAY

Thank God for all the freedoms you are enjoying. In particular, thank him for setting us free from guilt, addictive power and death.
Thank him for setting us free to love God and our neighbour and to be our true selves as God intended us to be.

LIFE'S GREAT RIDDLE

ECCLESIASTES 1:12 – 2:11

Wisdom Is Meaningless

[12]I, the Teacher, was king over Israel in Jerusalem. [13]I devoted myself to study and to explore by wisdom all that is done under heaven. What a heavy burden God has laid on the human race! [14]I have seen all the things that are done under the sun; all of them are meaningless, a chasing after the wind.

[15]What is twisted cannot be
straightened;
what is lacking cannot be counted.

[16]I thought to myself, "Look, I have grown and increased in wisdom more than anyone who has ruled over Jerusalem before me; I have experienced much of wisdom and knowledge." [17]Then I applied myself to the understanding of wisdom, and also of madness and folly, but I learned that this, too, is a chasing after the wind.

[18]For with much wisdom comes
much sorrow;
the more knowledge, the more
grief.

Pleasures Are Meaningless

2 I thought in my heart, "Come now, I will test you with pleasure to find out what is good." But that also proved to be meaningless. [2]"Laughter," I said, "is foolish. And what does pleasure accomplish?" [3]I tried cheering myself with wine, and embracing folly—my mind still guiding me with wisdom. I wanted to see what was worthwhile for people to do under heaven during the few days of their lives.

[4]I undertook great projects: I built houses for myself and planted vineyards. [5]I made gardens and parks and planted all kinds of fruit trees in them. [6]I made reservoirs to water groves of flourishing trees. [7]I bought male and female slaves and had other slaves who were born in my house. I also owned more herds and flocks than anyone in Jerusalem before me. [8]I amassed silver and gold for myself, and the treasure of kings and provinces. I acquired male and female singers, and a harem as well—the delights of the human heart. [9]I became greater by far than anyone in Jerusalem before me. In all this my wisdom stayed with me.

[10]I denied myself nothing my eyes
desired;
I refused my heart no pleasure.
My heart took delight in all my
work, and this was the reward
for all my labour.
[11]Yet when I surveyed all that my
hands had done
and what I had toiled to
achieve,
everything was meaningless, a
chasing after the wind;
nothing was gained under the
sun.

Wisdom and Folly Are Meaningless

[12]Then I turned my thoughts to
consider wisdom,
and also madness and folly.
What more can the king's successor
do
than what has already been done?
[13]I saw that wisdom is better than
folly,

'He's trying to find his way in a crazy world – just like we all are.'
This is how John McEnroe summed up the life of Bjorn Borg, five
times Wimbledon tennis champion and McEnroe's former rival.

People are searching for meaning in life. Albert Camus, the
French novelist, essayist and playwright said, 'Man cannot live
without meaning.' The writer of Ecclesiastes, in the shoes of the
great King Solomon, 3,000 years ago, speaks about the search
for meaning without God. He looks at three secular philosophies
which all have their modern equivalent.

1. ENLIGHTENMENT (1:12–18)
He searches for 'wisdom' and 'knowledge'. There is nothing wrong
with this; indeed reason and science are vital and complementary
to the Christian faith. But they only answer the 'when?' and 'how?'
questions – not the 'who?' and 'why?' To seek knowledge apart
from God can only be a 'chasing after the wind'.

True wisdom is found in a relationship with God through Jesus
Christ. The apostle Paul tells us that in him 'are hidden all the
treasures of wisdom and knowledge' (Colossians 2:3).

2. ENJOYMENT (2:1–3, 8, 10)
Hedonism is the doctrine that
pleasure is the chief good and
proper end of human beings. It
can be a form of escapism. The
writer tries laughter (v. 2). There
is nothing wrong with that but
it does not provide meaning.
He tries stimulants (v. 3). Many
try to escape through drink or
drugs. Then he tries music (v. 8).
Then sexual pleasure (v. 8b). In
fact Solomon had 700 wives and

"I'm number 698 you clever, rich, famous, fulfilled hunk you"

300 mistresses! Yet all this still did not satisfy (v. 11).

> *Innocent pleasures in moderation can provide relaxation for the*
> *body and mind and can foster family and other relationships.*
> *But pleasure, per se, offers no deep, lasting satisfaction or*
> *sense of fulfilment. The pleasure-centred person, too soon*
> *bored with each succeeding level of 'fun', constantly cries for*
> *more and more. So the next new pleasure has to be bigger and*
> *better, more exciting, with a bigger 'high'. A person in this state*
> *becomes almost entirely narcissistic, interpreting all of life in*
> *terms of the pleasure it provides to the self here and now.*
>
> *Seven Habits of Highly Effective People*, Stephen R. Covey, Simon & Schuster,
> 2004, p. 115

The more you seek it, the less you find it. True joy and pleasure are
found in a relationship with God. As the psalmist writes:

> *'You will fill me with joy in your presence, with eternal*
> *pleasures at your right hand.'*
>
> Psalm 16:11

3. ENRICHMENT (2:4–11)

Materialism is a tendency to prefer material possessions to
spiritual values. In his search for meaning the writer tries
building projects (v. 4), houses (vv. 4–5), having a large staff (v. 7),
possessions (v. 7b), money (v. 8), greatness, success and fame
(v. 9), work and career (v. 10b). Yet none of this satisfies (see
Ecclesiastes 5:10–11).

Enrichment is to be found not in materialism but in Christ.
The apostle Paul discovered for himself that everything else
was 'rubbish' compared to Christ. He wrote, 'Whatever was
to my profit I now consider loss for the sake of Christ. What is
more I consider everything a loss compared to the surpassing

greatness of knowing Christ Jesus my Lord, for whose sake I have lost all things. I consider them rubbish, that I may gain Christ...' (Philippians 3:7–8).

Ecclesiastes raises questions that the New Testament answers. Meaning is to be found not 'under the sun' but 'in the Son'. If we seek enlightenment, enjoyment and enrichment for and by themselves, they will be as elusive as the wind. We will never find them. But if we seek God, we will find them all. Jesus said, 'Seek first his kingdom and his righteousness, and all these things will be given to you as well' (Matthew 6:33).

What are your goals in life? Why not decide today to make your first ambition 'his kingdom and his righteousness'? Then you will find true wisdom, solid joy and lasting riches.

67

✋ PRAY

O most merciful redeemer, friend and brother, may we know you more clearly, love you more dearly, and follow you more nearly, day by day.
Richard of Chichester 1197–1253

DAY 14

WHAT SHALL I CHOOSE TO LIVE FOR?

JOSHUA 24:14-24

'When Balak son of Zippor, the king of Moab, prepared to fight against Israel, he sent for Balaam son of Beor to put a curse on you. ¹⁰But I would not listen to Balaam, so he blessed you again and again, and I delivered you out of his hand.

¹¹" 'Then you crossed the Jordan and came to Jericho. The citizens of Jericho fought against you, as did also the Amorites, Perizzites, Canaanites, Hittites, Girgashites, Hivites and Jebusites, but I gave them into your hands. ¹²I sent the hornet ahead of you, which drove them out before you—also the two Amorite kings. You did not do it with your own sword and bow. ¹³So I gave you a land on which you did not toil and cities you did not build; and you live in them and eat from vineyards and olive groves that you did not plant.'

¹⁴"Now fear the Lord and serve him with all faithfulness. Throw away the gods your ancestors worshipped beyond the River and in Egypt, and serve the Lord. ¹⁵But if serving the Lord seems undesirable to you, then choose for yourselves this day whom you will serve, whether the gods your ancestors served beyond the River, or the gods of the Amorites, in whose land you are living. But as for me and my household, we will serve the Lord."

¹⁶Then the people answered, "Far be it from us to forsake the Lord to serve other gods! ¹⁷It was the Lord our God himself who brought us and our parents up out of Egypt, from that land of slavery, and performed those great signs before our eyes. He protected us on our entire journey and among all the nations through which we travelled. ¹⁸And the Lord drove out before us all the nations, including the Amorites, who lived in the land. We too will serve the Lord, because he is our God."

¹⁹Joshua said to the people, "You are not able to serve the Lord. He is a holy God; he is a jealous God. He will not forgive your rebellion and your sins. ²⁰If you forsake the Lord and serve foreign gods, he will turn and bring disaster on you and make an end of you, after he has been good to you."

²¹But the people said to Joshua, "No! We will serve the Lord."

²²Then Joshua said, "You are witnesses against yourselves that you have chosen to serve the Lord."

"Yes, we are witnesses," they replied.

²³"Now then," said Joshua, "throw away the foreign gods that are among you and yield your hearts to the Lord, the God of Israel."

²⁴And the people said to Joshua, "We will serve the Lord our God and obey him."

²⁵On that day Joshua made a covenant for the people, and there at Shechem he drew up for them decrees and laws. ²⁶And Joshua recorded these things in the Book of the Law of God. Then he took a large stone and set it up there under the oak near the holy place of the Lord.

²⁷"See!" he said to all the people. "This stone will be a witness against us. It has heard all the words the Lord has said to us. It will be a witness against you if you are untrue to your God."

Life is full of choices. What we choose to live for is the most important choice of all. It faces every human being and affects every aspect of our life. Once we have made this choice, it will help us to make every other choice in life.

Joshua, Moses' successor as leader of the Israelites, at the end of his life, summons all the people with him and tells them they have to choose how to spend the rest of their lives. He says, 'choose for yourselves this day whom you will serve' (v. 15).

1. WHY DO WE HAVE TO CHOOSE?

Everyone is a servant – either voluntarily or involuntarily. Some people say, 'I am free. I don't serve anyone.' But that is not one of the options. We either serve 'the Lord' or 'foreign gods'. The gods referred to claimed to be modern and scientific with control over agriculture, sex and fertility. 'Other gods' in our context are any activities, habits or attitudes which lead us away from the Lord, such as materialism, promiscuity or self-centredness. Serving other gods leads eventually to emptiness, guilt and death. It reduces our ability to control our own lives, the very opposite of what it promises. Serving the Lord leads to freedom and the ability to make the right decisions for ourselves and our families.

69

2. WHY SHOULD WE CHOOSE THE LORD?

Joshua's answer is that they should choose God because of what he has done for them: his call, gifts, deliverance, defeat of their enemies and the promises he has fulfilled (vv. 17–18). From our perspective, God has sent his son Jesus to die for us and his Spirit to come and give us new life. He has liberated us from guilt, addiction, fear and death. He has set us free to know God, to love and to be transformed into his likeness.

3. WHAT DOES IT MEAN TO CHOOSE TO SERVE HIM?

Joshua says they must 'serve him with all faithfulness' (v. 14).
Literally the word means 'fulness', 'completeness', 'integrity'.
These people thought they could serve the Lord and keep the
other gods as well. But serving the Lord involves all our hearts
and all our lives.

" How about one day on, one day off sort of thing?"

4. HOW DO WE CHOOSE TO SERVE HIM?

Joshua's answer (v. 23) is two-fold:

'throw away the foreign gods'

Make sure that God has no rivals for his affection. In the words
of Dag Hammarskjöld, 'You cannot play with the animal in you
without becoming wholly animal, play with falsehood without
forfeiting your right to truth, play with cruelty without losing your
sensitivity of mind. He who wants to keep his garden tidy doesn't
reserve a plot for weeds' (*Markings*, translated by W. H. Auden and
Leif Sjoberg, Faber & Faber, 1966, p. 36).

'yield your hearts to the Lord'

We need to put every area of our lives into the hands of the Lord:
our family, friends, time, work, money, sexuality, possessions and
abilities.

In Joshua 1:1, Moses is described as 'a servant of the Lord' and Joshua as his assistant. In Joshua 24:29, Joshua is described as 'the servant of the Lord'. The apostle Paul was proud to describe himself as 'a servant of Jesus Christ'. Jesus saw himself as 'the suffering servant' of Isaiah 53. To be a servant of God is the highest calling a person can ever receive. Each of us can have this title – 'servant of the Lord' – if we choose to go on serving him throughout our lives.

🖐 PRAY

Why not ask God to reveal if there are any 'other gods' in your life? If there are, you could resolve today to get rid of them. Choose today to serve the Lord for the rest of your life. You will never regret it.

71

THE PURSUIT OF HAPPINESS

1 PETER 1:3-9

1 Peter, an apostle of Jesus Christ,

To God's elect, strangers in the world, scattered throughout Pontus, Galatia, Cappadocia, Asia and Bithynia, [2]who have been chosen according to the foreknowledge of God the Father, through the sanctifying work of the Spirit, for obedience to Jesus Christ and sprinkling by his blood:

Grace and peace be yours in abundance.

Praise to God for a Living Hope

[3]Praise be to the God and Father of our Lord Jesus Christ! In his great mercy he has given us new birth into a living hope through the resurrection of Jesus Christ from the dead, [4]and into an inheritance that can never perish, spoil or fade—kept in heaven for you, [5]who through faith are shielded by God's power until the coming of the salvation that is ready to be revealed in the last time. [6]In this you greatly rejoice, though now for a little while you may have had to suffer grief in all kinds of trials. [7]These have come so that your faith—of greater worth than gold, which perishes even though refined by fire—may be proved genuine and may result in praise, glory and honour when Jesus Christ is revealed. [8]Though you have not seen him, you love him; and even though you do not see him now, you believe in him and are filled with an inexpressible and glorious joy, [9]for you are receiving the goal of your faith, the salvation of your souls.

[10]Concerning this salvation, the prophets, who spoke of the grace that was to come to you, searched intently and with the greatest care, [11]trying to find out the time and circumstances to which the Spirit of Christ in them was pointing when he predicted the sufferings of Christ and the glories that would follow. [12]It was revealed to them that they were not serving themselves but you, when they spoke of the things that have now been told you by those who have preached the gospel to you by the Holy Spirit sent from heaven. Even angels long to look into these things.

Be Holy

[13]Therefore, prepare your minds for action; be self-controlled; set your hope fully on the grace to be given you when Jesus Christ is revealed. [14]As obedient children, do not conform to the evil desires you had when you lived in ignorance. [15]But just as he who called you is holy, so be holy in all you do; [16]for it is written: "Be holy, because I am holy."

[17]Since you call on a Father who judges each person's work impartially, live your lives as strangers here in reverent fear. [18]For you know that it was not with perishable things such as silver or gold that you were redeemed from the empty way of life handed down to you from your ancestors, [19]but with the precious blood of Christ, a lamb without blemish or defect. [20]He was chosen before the creation of the world, but was revealed in these last times for your sake. [21]Through him you believe in God, who raised him from the dead and glorified him, and so your faith and hope are in God.

[22]Now that you have purified yourselves by obeying the truth so that

All of us want to be happy. Peter tells us here how to find true happiness, how to be 'filled with an inexpressible and glorious joy' (v. 8). What causes happiness? How can we find this joy?

In David Myers' book, *The Pursuit of Happiness* (Avon Books Inc., 1993), he concludes that happy people have three things: 1. an optimistic outlook, 2. high self-esteem and 3. close relationships.

Where do we find these? The apostle Peter tells us in this passage.

1. AN OPTIMISTIC OUTLOOK (VV. 3-5)

What does the future hold for us? Peter praises God for the possibility of 'new birth' into a 'living hope' (v. 3). Biblical hope is not hazy but certain, growing in strength year by year.

When we 'hope it'll be a nice day,' we have no idea if it will be or not. However, when the Bible speaks of hope, it speaks of certainty because this hope is based on the resurrection of Jesus Christ, which really did happen. In a real place in Palestine, there is a real grave which is empty forever. Jesus Christ conquered death and is alive for eternity. Those who are born again through faith in Jesus Christ will do the same. Our future is entirely secure: we are 'shielded by God's power' for eternity (v. 5). This is a hope that far exceeds the hopes of this world.

Our inheritance is 'ready to be revealed'. We are like children waiting for our Christmas present without knowing exactly when Christmas will come. Normally we receive an inheritance when someone else dies and when we die we leave one. But this inheritance we receive in full when we die. It will 'never spoil' whereas everything we see around us here on earth will eventually perish. Our possessions here fade but this inheritance will never fade. It is 'kept in heaven' for us (v. 4).

Our heavenly inheritance is 'stored up' for us, reserved in our name (v. 4) and guaranteed. God is watching over us, as he will do forever.

73

2. HIGH SELF-ESTEEM (VV. 6-7)

The Old Testament prophesied that we would 'walk with heads held high' (Leviticus 26:13). How is this possible? Because we are forgiven by 'his great mercy' (v. 3). Life is not always easy. We may have to go through 'various trials' (v. 6) but Peter writes that within and beyond the pain and suffering, there is cause for rejoicing.

Why? First, because of the relative brevity of our trials in contrast with eternity: only 'a little while' (v. 6) – just like the pains of childbirth. Second, the results of the trials are that our faith is refined (v. 7) as gold is refined by fire and proved to be genuine, which ultimately will result in 'praise, glory and honour'. This refers to our praise and worship of God, but here it may also mean that God will give praise to his servants (eg see Matthew 25:14-30).

74

3. CLOSE RELATIONSHIPS (VV. 8-9)

At the core of our being there is a powerful longing for love and relationship.

Geri Halliwell has spoken often of her burning desire for fame which, once fulfilled, turned into the terrible fear of losing it. Now despite her fame and success, she says, (speaking for many): 'I just want to be happy... Yet, I feel really lonely, I want love in my life.'

The apostle Peter had seen Jesus. His listeners had not. They believed without having seen him, but they longed to see him and know him.

Larry King is a former CNN talk show host who has interviewed many of the richest, most famous, most influential people in the world. He said this: 'Jesus Christ had a more profound effect on mankind than any individual ever born. If there is one person in history I would like to interview, it would be Jesus.'

Maybe we feel the same. We would love to ask him all our unanswered questions. We can. We can know him now and love him now. The word used for love here implies a continual regular activity – a personal daily relationship with the ascended Lord Jesus. A personal trust in Christ and love for him is the reason for our greatest joy. This surely is the secret of happiness. This is the ultimate close relationship. The other two headings stem from it.

We can thank God today for the inheritance waiting in heaven for us to enjoy forever. This will help get our current problems and anxieties in perspective. If we are going through difficult times, we can pray that God will sustain us by his Spirit and use the experience to give us a deeper understanding of ourselves and of himself.

75

✍ PRAY

Join with the apostle Peter in praising the God and Father of our Lord Jesus Christ. Praise him for his great mercy, for your new birth, for your hope, for the resurrection of Jesus, for God's power shielding you and all the other blessings mentioned in this passage. Thank him for his love for you and tell him how much you love him. Ask him to fill you today with 'an inexpressible and glorious joy' and pray for your friends, family, neighbours and work colleagues that they may come to know this love and joy in their own lives.

FREEDOM FROM ADDICTION
ROMANS 6:1–14

16Again, the gift of God is not like the result of the one man's sin: The judgment followed one sin and brought condemnation, but the gift followed many trespasses and brought justification.

17For if, by the trespass of the one man, death reigned through that one man, how much more will those who receive God's abundant provision of grace and of the gift of righteousness reign in life through the one man, Jesus Christ.

18Consequently, just as the result of one trespass was condemnation for all people, so also the result of one act of righteousness was justification that brings life for all people. 19For just as through the disobedience of the one man the many were made sinners, so also through the obedience of the one man the many will be made righteous.

20The law was added so that the trespass might increase. But where sin increased, grace increased all the more, 21so that, just as sin reigned in death, so also grace might reign through righteousness to bring eternal life through Jesus Christ our Lord.

Dead to Sin, Alive in Christ

6 What shall we say, then? Shall we go on sinning, so that grace may increase? 2By no means! We died to sin; how can we live in it any longer? 3Or don't you know that all of us who were baptised into Christ Jesus were baptised into his death? 4We were therefore buried with him through baptism into death in order that, just as Christ was raised from the dead through the glory of the Father, we too may live a new life.

5If we have been united with him like this in his death, we will certainly also be united with him in his resurrection. 6For we know that our old self was crucified with him so that the body of sin might be done away with, that we should no longer be slaves to sin—7because anyone who has died has been freed from sin.

8Now if we died with Christ, we believe that we will also live with him. 9For we know that since Christ was raised from the dead, he cannot die again; death no longer has mastery over him. 10The death he died, he died to sin once for all; but the life he lives, he lives to God.

11In the same way, count yourselves dead to sin but alive to God in Christ Jesus. 12Therefore do not let sin reign in your mortal body so that you obey its evil desires. 13Do not offer the parts of your body to sin, as instruments of wickedness, but rather offer yourselves to God, as those who have been brought from death to life; and offer the parts of your body to him as instruments of righteousness. 14For sin shall not be your master, because you are not under law, but under grace.

Slaves to Righteousness

15What then? Shall we sin because we are not under law but under grace? By no means! 16Don't you know that when you offer yourselves to someone as obedient slaves, you are slaves to the one whom you obey—whether you are slaves to sin, which leads to death, or to obedience, which leads to righteousness? 17But thanks be to God that, though you used to be slaves to sin, you wholeheartedly obeyed the form of teaching to which you were entrusted.

At 10.56 on the night of 20 July 1969 our world changed forever. Two Americans, Neil Armstrong and Buzz Aldrin, walked on the moon. One of the greatest events of the twentieth century took place as the result of the lunar voyage of Apollo 11. To get there, the astronauts had to break out of the gravity pull of the earth. More energy was spent in the first few minutes of lift-off, in the first few miles of travel, than was used over the next days to travel half a million miles.

Habits and addictions have tremendous gravity pull. Breaking deeply embedded habitual tendencies such as procrastination, impatience, a critical spirit or selfishness involves more than a little will power and a few minor changes in our lives. 'Lift-off' takes a tremendous effort but, once we break out of the gravity pull, our freedom takes on a whole new dimension.

It is said that the only exercise some people take is jumping to the wrong conclusions. Having spoken in Romans 1–5 of forgiveness, justification by faith and the righteousness of God (that it is possible to be put right with God however bad we have been), Paul now fears that some of his readers will jump to the wrong conclusion and say, 'It does not matter if we continue to sin.'

Some go on sinning voluntarily. Rasputin, the mad monk and evil genius, taught his followers to go and sin so that God could forgive and they could experience more of God's love. Others do so involuntarily. They have some habit they can't get rid of. It could be alcoholism, drugs, materialism, anger, bad temper, some sexual sin, kleptomania, greed, lying or something else.

Whatever category we are in, the question is, 'Shall we continue?' Paul's answer is, 'By no means.' This passage raises three vital questions.

1. WHAT DO WE SEE WHEN WE LOOK AT THE CROSS? (VV. 1–10)

Paul's argument is that we cannot continue to sin because we have died! Our baptism signifies the fact that when Jesus died on the cross, we died (v. 3). When Jesus was buried, we were buried. When Jesus was raised, we were raised (v. 4). Our old self has been crucified (v. 6). Therefore, 'we should no longer be slaves to sin' (v. 6).

Bishop Taylor-Smith, former chaplain-general to the forces, asked a young man, 'When you think about the cross of Christ, what do you see?' He answered, 'I see Christ and two thieves.' The bishop asked, 'What else do you see?' He replied, 'I see the soldiers gambling... What are you fishing for?' The bishop replied, 'If that is all you see, I think you will have trouble with the Christian life. When I see the cross, with all that, I see the old Bishop Taylor-Smith. I was crucified with Christ.' Becoming a Christian involves a radical change. It is not a little addition. It is a new life.

2. WHAT DO YOU SEE WHEN YOU LOOK AT YOURSELF? (V. 11)

Paul writes, 'In the same way, count yourselves dead to sin but alive to God in Christ Jesus.' This involves a radical new self-image. I died on 16 February 1974. My old self died and then a new creation came into being, alive to God and freed from the power of sin. We do not need to say, 'I am an alcoholic because my father was' or, 'I am bad-tempered because my mother was.' We can be different. We need to see ourselves in a new way. We need a radical change in self-perception.

St Augustine lived a wild and immoral life. At the age of thirty-two he was converted in answer to his mother's prayers.

Shortly after his conversion he saw a woman he used to know. The moment he saw her he ran away. She called out, 'Augustine! Don't you recognise me? It's me!' He replied, 'I know it's you, but it's no longer me!'

3. HOW DO WE ACT ON WHAT WE SEE? (VV. 12–13)

As the theologian Bishop Lesslie Newbigin wrote, 'Everyone who has honestly faced the cross of Christ knows what is meant by this dying with Christ and knows that it is a reality, a deep and costly reality. And yet he knows also that the self which has died is still alive and has to be continually fought to the death. He knows that the new life in Christ which he has received is something which has to be daily put on again' (Lesslie Newbigin, *The Household of God*, SCM Press, p. 119).

It is not instant holiness, but a lifelong process. We do not need to continue in addictive patterns of sin. Once we have seen the truth and believed it, we need to act on it. We will still be tempted. We need to resist, fight, refuse, stop it. We must not give in. We must surrender ourselves to God to be used for his purposes. Christians do sin. However, Jesus enables us to be forgiven and return to the right path. For we are no longer enslaved to sin but have been freed to live a brand new life for God.

🖤 PRAY

Look at the cross of Christ again today. Picture yourself dying with Christ, being buried and rising with him to a new life. See yourself as you are: a new creation, free from the ingrained patterns of the past. Ask for the Holy Spirit's help to live like the new person you truly are.

WHAT IS FAITH?

HEBREWS 11:23-29

[11]By faith Abraham, even though he was past age—and Sarah herself was barren—was enabled to become a father because he considered him faithful who had made the promise. [12]And so from this one man, and he as good as dead, came descendants as numerous as the stars in the sky and as countless as the sand on the seashore.

[13]All these people were still living by faith when they died. They did not receive the things promised; they only saw them and welcomed them from a distance. And they admitted that they were aliens and strangers on earth. [14]People who say such things show that they are looking for a country of their own. [15]If they had been thinking of the country they had left, they would have had opportunity to return. [16]Instead, they were longing for a better country—a heavenly one. Therefore God is not ashamed to be called their God, for he has prepared a city for them.

[17]By faith Abraham, when God tested him, offered Isaac as a sacrifice. He who had received the promises was about to sacrifice his one and only son, [18]even though God had said to him, "It is through Isaac that your offspring will be reckoned." [19]Abraham reasoned that God could raise the dead, and figuratively speaking, he did receive Isaac back from death.

[20]By faith Isaac blessed Jacob and Esau in regard to their future.

[21]By faith Jacob, when he was dying, blessed each of Joseph's sons, and worshipped as he leaned on the top of his staff.

[22]By faith Joseph, when his end was near, spoke about the exodus of the Israelites from Egypt and gave instructions about his bones.

[23]By faith Moses' parents hid him for three months after he was born, because they saw he was no ordinary child, and they were not afraid of the king's edict.

[24]By faith Moses, when he had grown up, refused to be known as the son of Pharaoh's daughter. [25]He chose to be ill-treated along with the people of God rather than to enjoy the pleasures of sin for a short time. [26]He regarded disgrace for the sake of Christ as of greater value than the treasures of Egypt, because he was looking ahead to his reward. [27]By faith he left Egypt, not fearing the king's anger; he persevered because he saw him who is invisible. [28]By faith he kept the Passover and the sprinkling of blood, so that the destroyer of the firstborn would not touch the firstborn of Israel.

[29]By faith the people passed through the Red Sea as on dry land; but when the Egyptians tried to do so, they were drowned.

[30]By faith the walls of Jericho fell, after the people had marched around them for seven days.

[31]By faith the prostitute Rahab, because she welcomed the spies, was not killed with those who were disobedient.

[32]And what more shall I say? I do not have time to tell about Gideon, Barak, Samson, Jephthah, David, Samuel and the prophets, [33]who through faith conquered kingdoms, administered justice, and gained what was promised; who shut the mouths of lions, [34]quenched the fury of the flames, and escaped the edge of the sword; whose weakness was turned to strength; and who became powerful in

Who is the greatest person who has ever lived? Any Christian would reply, 'Jesus Christ.' If you had asked a Jew that question they would have replied, without doubt, 'Moses.' To the Jews, Moses was the supreme figure of history. He had rescued them from slavery and given them the law.

In this letter the writer found it necessary to prove to these Jewish Christians that Jesus was greater than Moses (Hebrews 3). Here he shows that Moses was and is pre-eminently a man of faith, high up on God's honours' list, raised up by God at a time when God's people were in great need.

81

Faith describes our relationship with God, which at heart is one of trust. Relationships depend on trust. The novelist Graham Greene wrote, 'It is impossible to go through life without trust – that would be to be imprisoned in the cell of one's own self.' The writer here alights on three aspects of Moses' faith:

1. FAITH AS CHOICE (VV. 23–26)
Moses had great advantages in life. He was physically good-looking (Exodus 2:2). He was brought up in the Egyptian royal household and received a first class education and training. He had the prospect of inheriting the great wealth of Egypt and experiencing all the pleasures of a royal prince, including as many

wives and mistresses as he chose. Jewish tradition suggests that he had the prospect of gaining the throne itself, probably the most powerful throne of the time.

But Moses had another great advantage: the faith of his parents (v. 23). He himself needed to make a choice. On the one hand, there was all that the world offered: money, sex and power. On the other, he could identify with God's people, a slave nation despised by well-educated Egyptians. Identifying with them meant danger, scorn and suffering. As he looked at this second alternative he saw something of 'greater value than the treasures of Egypt' (v. 26): the reward that God offers. He saw that whereas the pleasures of this world are fleeting (v. 25), God offers a lasting reward. Weighing the issues of time in the balance of eternity, he did what was absurd without God but wise with him.

He decided to throw his weight in with God's people. He chose to follow the Lord. It involved Moses trusting the Lord enough to say (in the terms of the schoolchild mnemonic of faith) '**F**orsaking **A**ll **I T**ake **H**im'. This is the justifying FAITH of the New Testament.

2. FAITH AS PERSEVERANCE (V. 27)

Twice Moses left Egypt. He left first as a criminal in flight after killing an Egyptian. The second time, he left as leader of the people of God. In between he persevered, showing courage, determination and endurance. Between the moment of choice and the moment of triumph there were many battles but he trusted God throughout. Another schoolchild mnemonic for faith is, 'Feeling Afraid, I Trust Him'. He trusted the invisible God before the very visible Pharaoh. Faith is persevering and trusting in 'him who is invisible' (v. 27).

3. FAITH REQUIRES EXPECTANCY (VV. 28–29)

Moses did what God told him to do. He had a conviction of God's power to kill and a belief that he would do what he had said. He believed that God could perform signs and wonders, the greatest of which was crossing the Red Sea (v. 29). Again faith involves trust. Perhaps this is the gift of faith which Paul speaks about (1 Corinthians 12:9) described by Professor Dunn as 'that mysterious "surge of confidence" which sometimes arises within a person in a particular situation' (J. Dunn, *Jesus and the Spirit*, Eerdmans, 1997, p. 211).

Our own faith begins with a choice, and often that choice involves giving things up. Then we need to stick at it, believing in God's power to work in our lives. There will be times when God gives us a special 'gift of faith' – a mysterious surge of confidence.

Thank God today for the example of Moses and pray that by the help of God's Holy Spirit you will be enabled to make the right choices, that you will persevere in your faith and that God will give you the 'gift of faith'.

⚘ PRAY

You might like to pray the prayer that Mother Teresa used to pray:

'Lord, increase my faith, bless my efforts and work, now and for evermore, Amen.'

HOW TO MAXIMISE YOUR POTENTIAL

MARK 4:1-20

[32]"Who are my mother and my brothers?" he asked.

[34]Then he looked at those seated in a circle around him and said, "Here are my mother and my brothers! [35]Whoever does God's will is my brother and sister and mother."

The Parable of the Sower

4 Again Jesus began to teach by the lake. The crowd that gathered round him was so large that he got into a boat and sat in it out on the lake, while all the people were along the shore at the water's edge. [2]He taught them many things by parables, and in his teaching said: [3]"Listen! A farmer went out to sow his seed. [4]As he was scattering the seed, some fell along the path, and the birds came and ate it up. [5]Some fell on rocky places, where it did not have much soil. It sprang up quickly, because the soil was shallow. [6]But when the sun came up, the plants were scorched, and they withered because they had no root. [7]Other seed fell among thorns, which grew up and choked the plants, so that they did not bear grain. [8]Still other seed fell on good soil. It came up, grew and produced a crop, multiplying thirty, sixty, or even a hundred times."

[9]Then Jesus said, "Those who have ears to hear, let them hear."

[10]When he was alone, the Twelve and the others around him asked him about the parables. [11]He told them, "The secret of the kingdom of God has been given to you. But to those on the outside everything is said in parables [12]so that,

'they may be ever seeing but
    never perceiving,
and ever hearing but never
    understanding;
otherwise they might turn and be
    forgiven!' "

[13]Then Jesus said to them, "Don't you understand this parable? How then will you understand any parable? [14]The farmer sows the word. [15]Some people are like seed along the path, where the word is sown. As soon as they hear it, Satan comes and takes away the word that was sown in them. [16]Others, like seed sown on rocky places, hear the word and at once receive it with joy. [17]But since they have no root, they last only a short time. When trouble or persecution comes because of the word, they quickly fall away. [18]Still others, like seed sown among thorns, hear the word; [19]but the worries of this life, the deceitfulness of wealth and the desires for other things come in and choke the word, making it unfruitful. [20]Others, like seed sown on good soil, hear the word, accept it, and produce a crop—thirty, sixty or even a hundred times what was sown."

A Lamp on a Stand

[21]He said to them, "Do you bring in a lamp to put it under a bowl or a bed? Instead, don't you put it on its stand? [22]For whatever is hidden is meant to be disclosed, and whatever is concealed is meant to be brought out into the open. [23]If any have ears to hear, let them hear.

[24]"Consider carefully what you hear," he continued. "With the measure you use,

Jesus often told stories to get people thinking. In this case, because the disciples didn't seem to understand the story, he explained it to them in detail. He said that the seed was the word of God and that the different soils represented different people. This parable may apply to all of us at different times in our lives.

There are four types of response to Jesus' message.

1. THE HARD-HEARTED (VV. 4, 15)

Some seed 'fell along the path' and 'the birds came and ate it up' (v. 4). Jesus explains that this represents people who hear the word but 'Satan comes and takes away the word that was sown in them' (v. 15). This is when we hear the word of God but it makes no deep impression. We do nothing about it. There are those who shrug off any mention of Christ with complete lack of interest. In effect, the devil has come and taken away the message.

85

2. THE FAINT-HEARTED (VV. 5-6, 16-17)

The seed lands on rocky ground with little soil and therefore the plant does not take root properly (vv. 5-6). The intense heat of the sun kills off the plant. Jesus explains that this soil represents those people who when they hear the word of God 'receive it with joy. But since there is no root, they last only a short time. When trouble or persecution come because of the word, they quickly fall away' (vv. 16-17). When something goes wrong in our life or we suffer ridicule or opposition, our enthusiasm for God fades because there is no root. The root is the part of our lives which no one sees: our secret life with God which gives strength to what appears above the surface.

3. THE HALF-HEARTED (VV. 7, 18-19)

Here the thorns grow faster than the wheat and therefore choke it (v. 7). Jesus said these thorns are first 'the worries of this life'. These could be job pressures, financial worries or concerns about one's family or even ministry. Second, the thorns are 'the deceitfulness of wealth', perhaps the desire for promotion at work, the grip of financial success or the blinding goal of becoming rich. Third, the thorns are 'the desire for other things' which can creep in and 'choke the word, making it unfruitful'. These things could be good in themselves (making a home, doing our job well, caring for children, keeping fit, putting time and energy into a relationship and so on) but if they distract us from following Christ we will be unfruitful.

4. THE WHOLE-HEARTED (VV. 8, 20)

The seed that falls on the good soil produces fruit thirty-fold, sixty-fold or even a hundred times what was sown (vv. 8, 20). The minimum is thirty times but they all had a very high output. These are the Christians who persevere and do not lose heart. We may feel that we have little to offer but the issue is not how much we have but what we do with what we have. If we hear God's word and respond to it throughout our lives we will produce a massive crop.

For most of us there have been times when we have not been wholehearted. This does not mean that we have to remain like that. We can repent of the times we have not responded to God, or when difficulties or opposition have overcome us or 'other things' have distracted us from following Christ.

What matters now is that we make the most of the rest of our lives – that we maximise our potential fruitfulness. We do this by constantly allowing the word of God to penetrate deeply into our lives – allowing him to speak to us through the Bible, as we pray, and through others in the Christian community.

Determine not to allow the difficulties or opposition to put you off. Beware of the 'other things' that can so easily creep in. Resolve to respond wholeheartedly to God's word, with the help of his Holy Spirit, throughout your life.

✒ PRAY

Commit yourself – heart, mind and body – everything you have to the Lord. Give yourself to him and ask him to give you the ability to 'hear his word, accept it and produce a crop' throughout the rest of your life.

RIGHT RELATIONSHIPS

JAMES 4:1–12

[10]Out of the same mouth come praise and cursing. My brothers and sisters, this should not be. [11]Can both fresh water and salt water flow from the same spring? [12]My brothers and sisters, can a fig-tree bear olives, or a grapevine bear figs? Neither can a salt spring produce fresh water.

Two Kinds of Wisdom

[13]Who are wise and understanding among you? Let them show it by their good life, by deeds done in the humility that comes from wisdom. [14]But if you harbour bitter envy and selfish ambition in your hearts, do not boast about it or deny the truth. [15]Such "wisdom" does not come down from heaven but is earthly, unspiritual, of the devil. [16]For where you have envy and selfish ambition, there you find disorder and every evil practice.

[17]But the wisdom that comes from heaven is first of all pure; then peace-loving, considerate, submissive, full of mercy and good fruit, impartial and sincere. [18]Peacemakers who sow in peace raise a harvest of righteousness.

Submit Yourselves to God

4 What causes fights and quarrels among you? Don't they come from your desires that battle within you? [2]You want something but don't get it. You kill and covet, but you cannot have what you want. You quarrel and fight. You do not have, because you do not ask God. [3]When you ask, you do not receive, because you ask with wrong motives, that you may spend what you get on your pleasures.

[4]You adulterous people, don't you know that friendship with the world is hatred towards God? Anyone who chooses to be a friend of the world becomes an enemy of God. [5]Or do you think Scripture says without reason that the spirit he caused to live in us envies intensely? [6]But he gives us more grace. That is why Scripture says:

"God opposes the proud
   but gives grace to the humble."

[7]Submit yourselves, then, to God. Resist the devil, and he will flee from you. [8]Come near to God and he will come near to you. Wash your hands, you sinners, and purify your hearts, you double-minded. [9]Grieve, mourn and wail. Change your laughter to mourning and your joy to gloom. [10]Humble yourselves before the Lord, and he will lift you up.

[11]Brothers and sisters, do not slander one another. Anyone who speaks against a brother or sister or judges them speaks against the law and judges it. When you judge the law, you are not keeping it, but sitting in judgment on it. [12]There is only one Lawgiver and Judge, the one who is able to save and destroy. But you—who are you to judge your neighbour?

Boasting About Tomorrow

[13]Now listen, you who say, "Today or tomorrow we will go to this or that city, spend a year there, carry on business and make money." [14]Why, you do not even know what will happen tomorrow. What is your life? You are a mist that appears for a little while and then vanishes. [15]Instead, you ought to say, "If it is the Lord's will, we will live and do this or that." [16]As it is, you boast and brag. All such boasting is evil.

James, the brother of Jesus, isolates three great problems facing the church and society. First, there is division – 'fights and quarrels' (vv. 1–3). Second, there is the problem of dissatisfied lives (v. 2). If we set our hearts on pleasure, as many do, we will never be satisfied. Third, we suffer from a lack of spiritual power (v. 3). How do we deal with these? The root of the problem is a breakdown of relationships. In this passage James urges us to get our relationships right.

"There is not a problem in the Church!"

89

1. RIGHT RELATIONSHIP WITH GOD (VV. 4–6)

James sees the Christian's relationship with God as akin to marriage, so that 'friendship with the world' (meaning the fallen world, organised in opposition to God) is the equivalent of adultery. The apostle John takes up this theme in 1 John 2, warning (in v. 15), 'Do not love the world or anything in the world.' In the following verse, he expands his point. The true purpose of our life is not to satisfy ourselves physically or materially nor to seek our identity in so-called success and worldly position. Those who seek satisfaction in these areas will never be satisfied because only a friendship with God can satisfy. God hates to see us go after other things (v. 5) and if we persist in doing so will oppose us (v. 6).

But if we humbly ask for his help he will give us his grace and his undeserved love. He is tirelessly on our side. God is so good that it is only reasonable to submit ourselves to him (v. 7). If we do so, we will desire what he desires and he will give us the desires of our hearts.

2. RIGHT RELATIONSHIP WITH EVIL (VV. 7–10)

We are called to fight the devil tooth and nail. The devil is the ruler of the world apart from God and wants to draw us away from this love relationship with God. He tries to drag us away through addiction, bad temper, theft, lust, lying, unforgiveness or some other sin. The battle is great but if we resist him, he flees (v. 7). As we draw near to God, he draws near to us (v. 8).

We are called to hate sin (vv. 8–9), to wash our hands and purify our hearts. We must put right what we do and what we think. We must not be 'double-minded' but have to decide between God and the world. In verse 9, James is not condemning all laughter. Laughter is healing and relieves stress and tension but we must not use complacent laughter where our actions call for regret and repentance (v. 9). As we humble ourselves he will lift us up (v. 10).

3. RIGHT RELATIONSHIPS WITH EACH OTHER (VV.11–12)

When we get right with God we will also want to be at peace with our brothers and sisters. James says, 'do not slander one another' (v. 11). Slander and backbiting are illustrations of a lack of humility. We bring others down in order to puff ourselves up.

Three times he speaks of our fellow Christians as brothers and sisters. In speaking evil we are failing to love our brothers and sisters. The law tells us to love one another. In speaking against one another, we are speaking against the law. In a negative and critical environment people shrivel up and die emotionally. The opposite is an atmosphere of love and encouragement which enables people to blossom. We demonstrate our love for God by the way we treat our brothers and sisters.

Christianity for James, as for Jesus, is about relationships. It is about loving God and loving others. It is about resisting anything which gets in the way. If we put our relationships right, all the rest will follow. We will find ourselves totally aligned to the will of God. If we love God and love our neighbour there is nothing that God will not do for us.

'Resist the devil, and he will flee from you. Come near to God and he will come near to you' (vv. 7–8). It is worth learning this by heart, meditating on it and using it whenever we are tempted.

*️ PRAY

Ask God for the strength to resist temptation – 'lead us not into temptation but deliver us from evil' – and pray that God will draw near to you as you draw near to him.

91

HOW CAN THE BIBLE BECOME A DELIGHT?

PSALM 1

PSALMS

BOOK I

Psalms 1–41

Psalm 1

¹Blessed are those
  who do not walk in the counsel
    of the wicked
  or stand in the way of sinners
    or sit in the seat of mockers.
²But their delight is in the law of
    the Lord,
  and on his law they meditate day
    and night.
³They are like trees planted by
    streams of water,
  which yield their fruit in season
and whose leaf does not wither.
  Whatever they do prospers.

⁴Not so the wicked!
  They are like chaff
  that the wind blows away.
⁵Therefore the wicked will not
    stand in the judgment,
  nor sinners in the assembly of
    the righteous.

⁶For the Lord watches over the
    way of the righteous,
  but the way of the wicked will
    perish.

Psalm 2

¹Why do the nations conspire
  and the peoples plot in vain?
²The kings of the earth take their
    stand and the rulers gather
    together against the Lord
  and against his Anointed One.
³"Let us break their chains," they say,
  "and throw off their fetters."

⁴The One enthroned in heaven
    laughs; the Lord scoffs at them.
⁵Then he rebukes them in his anger
  and terrifies them in his wrath,
    saying,
⁶"I have installed my King
  on Zion, my holy hill."

⁷I will proclaim the decree of the
  Lord:

He said to me, "You are my Son;
  today I have become your Father.
⁸Ask of me,
  and I will make the nations your
    inheritance,
  the ends of the earth your
    possession.
⁹You will rule them with an iron
    scepter;
  you will dash them to pieces like
    pottery."

Marion was studying English at university. In the second term she had to write an essay on a particular modern writer. She found his work boring: she could not get into his novels or short stories and the deadline for her essay loomed closer and closer with very little achieved.

Glad to have the chance to get away from her largely fruitless studies, she went with some of her friends to a party at their tutor's home. During the evening her tutor introduced her to a very good-looking man in his early thirties.
He seemed to know a lot about literature and was extremely interesting. Marion was captivated by him. During the conversation, Marion discovered him to be the modern writer who was the subject of her essay. That night she went home and in the small hours started to read page after page of his work and found it absolutely fascinating. (*Drive the Point Home*, Graham Twelftree, Monarch 1994, p. 38)

Once we know the author of the Bible, it too can become an exciting book. The psalmist says that 'their delight is in the law of the Lord' (v. 2). All he had at this stage were the first five books of the Bible. They were his delight. He encourages us to do as he did – 'to meditate day and night' (v. 2) – which involves reading and thinking about the Bible regularly. Perhaps set aside a particular time each day to study God's word.

The psalmist encourages us that if we delight in the law of the Lord in this way, then certain things will happen in our lives.

1. WE SHALL PRODUCE FRUIT

He says, 'They are like trees planted by streams of water, which yield their fruit in season' (v. 3). This promise is that as we immerse ourselves in the Bible, our life will produce fruit, the fruit of the Spirit. Not only will our own life change but this fruit will include the transformation of other people's lives. It is not only for our benefit that we read the Bible but so that we can be a blessing to others: our friends, colleagues, neighbours and the society in which we live. This is the fruit that will last into eternity (John 15:16).

2. WE SHALL PERSEVERE

The second promise given to those whose delight is in the law of the Lord is that they will be like trees whose 'leaves do not wither' (v. 3). If we stay close to Jesus Christ through his word, we will not dry up or lose our spiritual vitality. It is not enough to have great spiritual experiences, although they are very important and very wonderful. Unless we are deeply rooted in Jesus Christ, in his word and in that relationship with him, we won't be able to withstand the storms of life. If we are rooted in that relationship and delighting in his word, then when the storms come we shall stand firm.

3. WE WILL PROSPER

The psalmist says that the person who delights in the word of God will prosper in whatever they do (v. 3). Our lives may not be ones of material prosperity, but we shall prosper in the ways that really matter in life: in our relationship with God, our relationships with others and the transforming of our characters into the likeness of Jesus Christ. These things are far more valuable than material wealth.

With the psalmist and millions of other Christians why not determine to make the Bible your delight? Decide today to make reading the Bible a high priority in your life. Read it every day, if possible. The promise of Scripture is that if you delight in the law of the Lord you will become like a tree planted by streams of water, you will yield 'fruit' in your life and you will prosper in whatever you do.

George Müller began a ministry that rescued hundreds of starving orphans from death in the slums of England. As important as his role was in showing these needy children the love of their heavenly Father, the ministry was never Müller's first priority. He believed God's highest call on his life was for intimate relationship with him.

God had shown him that the way to have this was through daily Bible meditation. He said, 'God showed me that I should go to his Word to chew on it early in the morning. This is not something I do for my ministry, but something for me personally, that I would be nourished.' History testifies to the tremendous impact this meditation had on his life and ministry. Imagine what God could accomplish through each of us if we started each day by meditating on the Bible.

95

🖐 PRAY

Thank God for the Bible and ask him to speak to you each day as you read it. Pray along with the psalmist, 'Open my eyes that I may see wonderful things in your law' (Psalm 119:18).

DEALING WITH GUILT

PSALM 51

Psalm 51

*For the director of music. A psalm of David.
When the prophet Nathan came to him
after David had committed adultery with
Bathsheba.*

¹Have mercy on me, O God,
  according to your unfailing love;
  according to your great compassion
  blot out my transgressions.
²Wash away all my iniquity
  and cleanse me from my sin.

³For I know my transgressions,
  and my sin is always before me.
⁴Against you, you only, have I
  sinned
  and done what is evil in your
  sight,
  so that you are proved right
  when you speak
  and justified when you judge.
⁵Surely I was sinful at birth,
  sinful from the time my mother
  conceived me.
⁶Surely you desire truth in the inner
  parts;
  you teach me wisdom in the
  inmost place.

⁷Cleanse me with hyssop, and I
  shall be clean;
  wash me, and I will be whiter than
  snow.
⁸Let me hear joy and gladness;
  let the bones you have crushed
  rejoice.
⁹Hide your face from my sins
  and blot out all my iniquity.

¹⁰Create in me a pure heart, O God,
  and renew a steadfast spirit
  within me.
¹¹Do not cast me from your
  presence
  or take your Holy Spirit from
  me.
¹²Restore to me the joy of your
  salvation
  and grant me a willing spirit, to
  sustain me.

¹³Then I will teach transgressors
  your ways,
  and sinners will turn back to you.
¹⁴Save me from bloodguilt, O God,
  the God who saves me,
  and my tongue will sing of your
  righteousness.
¹⁵O Lord, open my lips,
  and my mouth will declare your
  praise.
¹⁶You do not delight in sacrifice, or
  I would bring it;
  you do not take pleasure in burnt
  offerings.
¹⁷The sacrifices of God are a
  broken spirit;
  a broken and contrite heart,
  O God, you will not despise.

¹⁸In your good pleasure make Zion
  prosper;
  build up the walls of Jerusalem.
¹⁹Then there will be righteous
  sacrifices,
  whole burnt offerings to delight
  you;
  then bulls will be offered on
  your altar.

What do we do when we have sinned and let God down? How do we get ourselves right with God? How do we receive his mercy?

King David wrote this psalm when he was racked by guilt after he had committed adultery with Bathsheba, then engineered the death of her husband and finally taken her to be his wife. All this was made public by the prophet Nathan, and the enormity of what he had done filled David with remorse (see 2 Samuel 11 onwards).

1. DAVID SAW THE NEED FOR GOD'S MERCY (VV. 1–5)

We cannot appreciate the mercy of God until we see our own need and the seriousness of our sin. David uses three words to describe his own wrongdoing.

Transgression (vv. 1, 3)

This means crossing a boundary. God's boundaries are there for our protection, security and enjoyment. When we cross them people get hurt. In one series of actions David had broken four commands. He was guilty of coveting, theft, adultery and murder. One sin had led to another.

> "David murdered; I stole sweets. So there is a chance"

Sin (v. 4)
This means missing the mark or falling short of a target. It is the difference between what we are and what we might have been. David recognises that he has sinned against God. The essence of sin is revolt against God. He does not try to justify himself (v. 4).

Iniquity (v. 5)
This points to the fact that our whole nature and character are flawed. Human nature is infected by sin. However, this is not incompatible with human responsibility. David accepts responsibility and does not make excuses for his actions. We cannot blame our parents, God, friends or even the devil. A man of mature years at the height of his career with great power and popularity is prepared to admit he is a sinner in need of God's mercy.

2. DAVID SAW THE GREATNESS OF GOD'S MERCY
He uses three expressions and three metaphors.

Library
He prays that God would 'blot out' his transgressions (v. 1). It is as if God has a book of guilt and will blot out the entries.

Laundry
The effect of sin is to make us dirty. David prays that God will wash him clean (v. 2).

Leprosy
David prays that God would 'cleanse me with hyssop' (v. 7). This was how a leper was cleansed. A bunch of hyssop was used to sprinkle sacrificial blood onto him seven times. Just as the healing of leprosy involves creation of new skin, so David prays, 'Create in me a pure heart, O God, and renew a steadfast spirit within me' (v. 10).

Only in the light of the cross can this be fully understood. Our sins have been blotted out because Jesus paid the price for them. We 'were washed... in the name of the Lord Jesus Christ and by the Spirit of our God' (1 Corinthians 6:11). The blood of Christ cleanses us from all sin (1 John 1:7 RSV).

3. DAVID SAW THE RESULTS OF GOD'S MERCY (V. 11 ONWARDS)
He did not escape all the tragic consequences of his sin (see 2 Samuel 12 and the rest of the history of Israel). However, David did recover much of what he had lost through his sin.

- His sense of the presence of God (v. 11)

- The power of the Holy Spirit in his life (v. 11)

- The joy of his salvation (v. 12)

- His enthusiasm for doing God's work (v. 12)

- The effectiveness of his ministry (v. 13)

- His intimacy with God (v. 15)

God in his mercy restored all this when David came and said, 'Have mercy on me.' God will never despise a 'broken and contrite heart' (v. 17). However serious our sin, God's mercy is even greater.

99

🤲 PRAY

Ask God to reveal to you if there is anything for which you need to ask God's forgiveness and then read this psalm as your own prayer to God.

OVERCOMING FEAR

PSALM 91

¹⁶May your deeds be shown to your
servants,
your splendour to their children.

¹⁷May the favour of the Lord our
God rest upon us;
establish the work of our hands
for us—
yes, establish the work of our
hands.

Psalm 91

¹Whoever dwells in the shelter of
the Most High
will rest in the shadow of the
Almighty.
²I will say of the LORD, "He is my
refuge and my fortress,
my God, in whom I trust."

³Surely he will save you from the
fowler's snare
and from the deadly pestilence.
⁴He will cover you with his
feathers,
and under his wings you will
find refuge;
his faithfulness will be your
shield and rampart.
⁵You will not fear the terror of
night,
nor the arrow that flies by day,
⁶nor the pestilence that stalks in the
darkness,
nor the plague that destroys at
midday.
⁷A thousand may fall at your side,
ten thousand at your right hand,
but it will not come near you.
⁸You will only observe with your
eyes

and see the punishment of the
wicked.

⁹If you make the Most High your
dwelling—
even the LORD, who is my
refuge—
¹⁰then no harm will befall you,
no disaster will come near your
tent.
¹¹For he will command his angels
concerning you
to guard you in all your ways;
¹²they will lift you up in their hands,
so that you will not strike your
foot against a stone.
¹³You will tread upon the lion and
the cobra;
you will trample the great lion
and the serpent.

¹⁴"Because you love me," says the
LORD, "I will rescue you;
I will protect him, for you
acknowledge my name.
¹⁵You will call upon me, and I will
answer you;
I will be with you in trouble,
I will deliver you and honour
you.
¹⁶With long life will I satisfy you
and show you my salvation."

Psalm 92
A psalm. A song. For the Sabbath day.

¹It is good to praise the LORD
and make music to your name,
O Most High,
²to proclaim your love in the morning
and your faithfulness at night,
³to the music of the ten-stringed lyre

A large and dangerous-looking fifty-year-old truck driver was asked on a candid camera TV interview: 'If you could be any age you wanted what age would you be?' There was a long silence and then he replied, 'Three. When you are three you don't have any responsibilities.' He was yearning for the feeling of childhood: the sense that you are loved, protected and perfectly safe. This is the sense, above all, that somebody else is in charge.

The fears of life are many and varied: the future, the dark, being laughed at or attacked, fear of HIV, bankruptcy, loneliness, growing old, death, singleness, relationships breaking up, illness, failure, occult powers, war and so on. However, the most common command in the Bible is, 'Do not fear.' It occurs 366 times in the Bible (one for each day and an extra one to cover leap years).

" oh no, now they say toothpaste is fattening "

101

Here, the psalmist expresses one of the many moods of faith. He is celebrating his own confidence in the sheltering providence of God. Perhaps he had just been protected by God in a dangerous situation. All of us (just like those we read about in Scripture) are likely to experience such times of joy and celebration, as well as times of sadness and frustration. Throughout the ups and downs of life, we know that no final harm can touch us because nothing can ever separate us from the love of God in the present or throughout eternity (Romans 8:35–39).

With that knowledge, the psalmist encourages us to live lives free from fear, stating in verses 9–10: 'If you make the Most High your dwelling... then no harm will befall you.' He is, of course, not saying that everything will turn out just as we want it to. It does not mean that we can avoid times of trouble – see verse 15. Faith in the sheltering wings of God does not remove physical danger or the need for precaution against it. However, every Christian has the assurance that God is involved in every detail of our lives for all of eternity.

1. THE PSALMIST TESTIFIES FROM HIS OWN EXPERIENCE (VV. 1–2)

Four names for God are given. He is 'the Most High' – everything is under his control. He is 'the Almighty' – the all-powerful one. He is 'the Lord' – the universe is subject to his lordship. He is 'my God' – he is in a personal relationship with those who follow him.

There are four metaphors of security. We are safe in his 'shelter', 'shadow', 'refuge' and 'fortress'. There are three positions of security: dwelling, abiding and trusting.

2. THE PSALMIST SPEAKS TO US (VV. 3–13)

In verses 3–6, he promises God's protection from every kind of danger, 'the snare of the fowler' and 'the deadly pestilence' (v. 3). Then he says that God is like an eagle protecting us under his wings, giving a picture of his tender love (v. 4). His faithfulness is a 'shield and rampart' (v. 4), a picture of military protection. He promises release from the 'terror of night' (v. 5) – the sudden fears, often out of proportion, that prevent us from sleeping. He also promises protection from sudden attacks or disasters (v. 6).

In verses 7–10, he promises God's individual protection from ultimate harm. If we love him (v. 14) nothing can take away our relationship with him. God is sovereign and loving. As Paul puts it in the New Testament, 'In all things God works for the good of those who love him, who have been called according to his purpose' (Romans 8:28).

In verses 11–13, he even promises miraculous protection saying that God promises that he will send his angels to look after us.

3. THE LORD HIMSELF SPEAKS (VV. 14–16)

He promises eight wonderful things: deliverance, protection, answered prayer, his presence, rescue, honour, long life (now 'eternal life') and most important of all, salvation.

Today, bring all your fears and anxieties to God in prayer. As the apostle Peter wrote, 'Cast all your anxiety on him because he cares for you' (1 Peter 5:7). It is not that we don't have any responsibilities nor that we can go through life without facing problems, difficulties and sadness. But it is possible to enjoy the security of childhood for ever. Someone else is in charge and, whatever happens, we can be sure that we are loved, protected and ultimately perfectly safe for ever.

🤚 PRAY

You might like to pray the prayer of St Augustine of Hippo (AD 354–430):

'O God, grant us in all our perplexities your guidance,
in all our dangers your protection,
and in all our sorrows your peace,
through Jesus Christ our Lord, Amen.'

SUCCESS

PROVERBS 16:1–9

³⁰A cheerful look brings joy to the
heart,
and good news gives health to the
bones.
³¹Whoever listens to a life-giving
rebuke
will be at home among the wise.

³²Those who ignore discipline
despise themselves,
but those who heed correction
gain understanding.

³³The fear of the Lord teaches
wisdom,
and humility comes before
honour.

16 To human beings belong the
plans of the heart,
but from the Lord comes the
reply of the tongue.

²People think all their ways are
innocent,
but motives are weighed by the
Lord.

³Commit to the Lord whatever you
do,
and your plans will succeed.

⁴The Lord works out everything
for his own ends—
even the wicked for a day of
disaster.

⁵The Lord detests all the proud of
heart.
Be sure of this: They will not go
unpunished.

⁶Through love and faithfulness sin
is atoned for;

through the fear of the Lord evil
is avoided.

⁷When people's ways are pleasing
to the Lord,
he makes even their enemies live
at peace with them.

⁸Better a little with righteousness
than much gain with injustice.

⁹In your heart you may plan your
course,
but the Lord determines your
steps.

¹⁰The lips of a king speak as an
oracle,
and his mouth should not betray
justice.

¹¹Honest scales and balances are
from the Lord;
all the weights in the bag are of
his making.

¹²Kings detest wrongdoing,
for a throne is established
through righteousness.

¹³Kings take pleasure in honest
lips;
they value one who speaks the
truth.

¹⁴A king's wrath is a messenger of
death,
but the wise will appease it.

¹⁵When a king's face brightens, it
means life;
his favour is like a rain cloud in
spring.

¹⁶How much better to get wisdom

Malcolm Muggeridge, in a *Twentieth-Century Testimony*, wrote:
'When I look back on my life nowadays, which I sometimes do,
what strikes me most forcibly about it is that what seemed at
that time most significant and seductive, seems now most futile
and absurd. For instance, success in all of its various guises;
being known and being praised; ostensible pleasures, like
acquiring money or seducing women, or travelling, going to and
fro in the world and up and down in it like Satan, explaining and
experiencing whatever Vanity Fair has to offer. In retrospect, all
these exercises in self-gratification seem pure fantasy, what
Pascal called, "licking the earth".'

Many people work harder and harder climbing the ladder of
success only to discover it's leaning against the wrong wall. If the
ladder is not leaning against the right wall, every step we take just
gets us to the wrong place faster.

True success comes from having God at the centre of every
aspect of our lives: our family, money, work, possessions, friends,
pleasure and so on. It is not wrong to plan ahead. It is assumed in
this passage that we will do so. We may have plans for our job, our
family, our church, our holidays and so on. Whatever our plans, we
want them to be a success. Here we see the secret of success. In
verse 3 there is a promise and a condition.

1. THE CONDITION OF SUCCESS

We are urged, 'Commit to the Lord whatever you do' (v. 3a). What
does this mean?

First, it means:

Surrendering our wills

There are two ways to go through life. Either we decide we are
perfectly capable of running our own lives. We don't need anyone
else – not even God. We make our own plans, without God, to
please ourselves. This leads to pride and independence (v. 5).

Alternatively, there is the way of faith. We believe that God wants the very best for our lives (Jeremiah 29:11; Ephesians 2:10). We know that we will not discover his plans until we humbly surrender our wills to him. That is what it means to become a Christian. We need to stay in that attitude daily, willing to give up anything which clashes with his plans.

Second, it means to:

Consult with God

This means making all our plans together with God. It may be a help each day to go through our diary committing each event to the Lord. Perhaps at the beginning of each year we might plan ahead with God. God will be concerned about anything of concern to us. We need not go to absurd extremes. We don't need to pray about whether to get up in the morning. Certain things are common sense. God does not intend us to be robots – he has given us freedom of choice within the parameters of his word.

which socks Lord?

2. THE PROMISE OF SUCCESS

The writer says, 'your plans will succeed' (v. 3b). What does this mean? God is sovereign (vv. 1, 4, 9). 'The Lord works out everything for his own ends' (v. 4). God works within events to bring about his purposes. This does not mean that only good things happen to us but that in and through everything, good and bad, 'The Lord works out everything for his own ends.' Or as St Paul puts it: 'In all things God works for the good of those who love him' (Romans 8:28). There are no loose ends with God. Everything is under his control. Doors may shut and there may be disappointments or doors may open in marvellous ways. Whatever happens, 'the Lord determines your steps' (v. 9).

God will work everything out for the good of those who love him (vv. 6b–7). This does not necessarily mean material prosperity or a life without difficulty (v. 8) but it does mean a successful life. True success lies in a right relationship with God and a right relationship with other people.

Success can be so dazzling. Many people think they would like a fast car, a smart house, loads of money, a touch of fame and the self-confidence these things appear to bring. However, God does not define success in these terms.

Look again at verses 5 and 8. You may want to pray that God would change your understanding of success. Then you will start to experience the thrill and fulfilment of true success: a growing relationship with the God who made us and right relationships with other people.

107

🖐 PRAY

You might like to begin today by committing to God all your plans for the future – short-term and long-term.

FORGIVENESS

MATTHEW 18:21–35

Dealing with Sin in the Church

¹⁵"If your brother or sister sins against you, go and show them their fault, just between the two of you. If they listen to you, you have won them over. ¹⁶But if they will not listen, take one or two others along, so that 'every matter may be established by the testimony of two or three witnesses.' ¹⁷If they refuse to listen to them, tell it to the church; and if they refuse to listen even to the church, treat them as you would a pagan or a tax collector.

¹⁸"I tell you the truth, whatever you bind on earth will be bound in heaven, and whatever you loose on earth will be loosed in heaven.

¹⁹"Again, I tell you that if two of you agree about anything you ask for, it will be done for you by my Father in heaven. ²⁰For where two or three come together in my name, there I am with them."

The Parable of the Unmerciful Servant

²¹Then Peter came to Jesus and asked, "Lord, how many times shall I forgive someone who sins against me? Up to seven times?"

²²Jesus answered, "I tell you, not seven times, but seventy-seven times.

²³"Therefore, the kingdom of heaven is like a king who wanted to settle accounts with his servants. ²⁴As he began the settlement, a man who owed him ten thousand talents was brought to him. ²⁵Since he was not able to pay, the master ordered that he and his wife and his children and all that he had be sold to repay the debt.

²⁶"The servant fell on his knees before him. 'Be patient with me,' he begged, 'and I will pay back everything.' ²⁷The servant's master took pity on him, cancelled the debt and let him go.

²⁸"But when that servant went out, he found one of his fellow-servants who owed him a hundred denarii. He grabbed him and began to choke him. 'Pay back what you owe me!' he demanded.

²⁹"His fellow-servant fell to his knees and begged him, 'Be patient with me, and I will pay you back.'

³⁰"But he refused. Instead, he went off and had the man thrown into prison until he could pay the debt. ³¹When the other servants saw what had happened, they were greatly distressed and went and told their master everything that had happened.

³²"Then the master called the servant in. 'You wicked servant,' he said, 'I cancelled all that debt of yours because you begged me to. ³³Shouldn't you have had mercy on your fellow-servant just as I had on you?' ³⁴In anger his master turned him over to the jailers to be tortured, until he should pay back all he owed.

³⁵"This is how my heavenly Father will treat each of you unless you forgive one another from your heart."

Divorce

19 When Jesus had finished saying these things, he left Galilee and went into the region of Judea to the other side of the Jordan. ²Large crowds followed him, and he healed them there.

³Some Pharisees came to him to test him. They asked, "Is it lawful for a man to

John Plummer was a helicopter pilot during the Vietnam War. He helped organise a napalm raid on the village of Trang Bang in 1972, a bombing immortalised by the prize-winning photograph of one of its victims. In the photo, Phan Thi Kim Phuc, a naked nine-year-old girl, burned, crying, arms outstretched, runs towards the camera with plumes of black smoke billowing in the sky behind her.

For twenty-four years his conscience tormented him. He badly wanted to find the girl to say that he was sorry. On Veterans' Day 1996, John met Kim at the Vietnam Memorial. Kim had come to Washington DC to lay a wreath for peace; John had come with a group of former pilots still searching for freedom from the past. In a speech to the crowd, Kim, now a Christian, said that she forgave the men who had bombed her village. John pushed through the crowds and managed to catch her attention.

He identified himself as the pilot responsible for bombing her village twenty-four years before, and they were able to talk for two short minutes. 'Kim saw my grief, my pain, my sorrow... She held out her arms to me and embraced me. All I could say was "I'm sorry; I'm sorry" – over and over again. And at the same time she was saying, "It's all right, I forgive you."'

They met again later the same day, and Kim reaffirmed her forgiveness. They have since become good friends, and call each other regularly. (See *The Lost Art of Forgiving*, Johann Christoph Arnold, Plough Publishing House, 1998.)

Forgiveness is never easy but it is vital. We are all human. We make mistakes and we hurt each other. Unforgiveness is at the root of so much anger, quarrelling, division, slander, gossip, arrogance and disorder (2 Corinthians 12:20). The teaching of Jesus in this passage is crucial for all relationships: for marriage, family life, church life, relationships at work and in the community and for our eternal destiny. We see three important things about forgiveness.

109

" Three times a minute, day, week or what?"

1. UNLIMITED FORGIVENESS IS COMMANDED BY JESUS (VV. 21–22)

The apostle Peter presumably had difficult relationships. He asked Jesus how many times he needed to forgive.

The Jewish teachers taught that we should forgive three times, at most four (on the basis of the book of Amos).

The apostle Peter offers to go further and forgive seven times. He believed in forgiveness. The Jews believed in it. Nearly everybody believes in forgiveness. They would say, 'It is right to forgive... up to a point. But there comes a point where a person has gone too far and we are justified in not forgiving.' The radical part of Jesus' teaching is that he requires unlimited forgiveness.

It does not mean that we condone sin as Christians, nor that there is no place for the law or for justice. The New Testament distinguishes the actions of the state from our responses in personal relationships (see Romans 13). What it does mean is that in our personal relationships we lay aside all malice, revenge and retribution. Forgiveness is hard, but it is possible.

2. UNLIMITED FORGIVENESS IS A REASONABLE RESPONSE TO THE UNLIMITED FORGIVENESS WE HAVE RECEIVED (VV. 23-30)

A talent was the highest unit of currency, equivalent to 6,000 denarii. The annual revenue from Galilee and Perea was 200 talents. The total revenue of a wealthy province might be 300 talents. 10,000 was the highest Greek numeral, and 10,000 talents was an immense amount, the highest figure imaginable – it was the equivalent for us of 'untold millions'.

In this story the servant was required to sell his family, not just to repay the debt but also as a form of public humiliation (v. 25). He pleads for time (v. 26), which is absurd. He could never pay the debt back. It is the hope of a desperate man. In verse 27 we see in the person of the servant's master what God is like. He does not simply give him time to pay.

He loves him and so is moved to show compassion by cancelling the debt and giving the whole family their freedom. He goes way beyond what is required by showing unlimited forgiveness. (We now know that all this is possible through what Jesus was about to do on the cross.)

Then the forgiven servant finds his fellow servant who owes him one six hundred thousandth of his debt and aggressively demands payment (v. 28). In this brilliant short story we side first with the underdog and then are shown the absurdity of a forgiven sinner standing on his rights. Next we find ourselves accusing not the man in the parable but ourselves. The only reasonable response to the unlimited forgiveness of God is unlimited forgiveness of others.

3. UNLIMITED FORGIVENESS IS NECESSARY IF WE WANT TO BE FORGIVEN (VV. 31-35)

The king turns the unforgiving servant over to the jailers 'to be tortured'. Unforgiveness tortures the soul.

The clear teaching of the New Testament is that we must

forgive (Matthew 5:7; Matthew 6:12, 14–15; James 2:13). We do not earn forgiveness. It is made possible through the cross. Our willingness to forgive is evidence that we know God's forgiveness. Once we recognise our need for unlimited forgiveness and have received it, we must forgive others 'from the heart', which means totally.

🖐 PRAY

Forgiveness is an act of the will. If there are those whose names come to mind as you read this, choose to forgive them and as an act of the will release them into God's hands. You will probably need to ask for God's help. If you are dealing with very painful issues, it may be wise to seek someone in leadership or a Christian you know and respect to pray with. Ask for God's help to make forgiveness a lifetime habit. We can forgive, not in our own strength but out of the overflow of forgiveness that God has shown us.

LONELINESS

found. ²¹So the Lord God caused the man to fall into a deep sleep; and while he was

sleeping, he took one of the man's ribs and closed up the place with flesh. ²²Then the Lord God made a woman from the rib he had taken out of the man, and he brought her to the man.

²³The man said,

"This is now bone of my bones
    and flesh of my flesh;
she shall be called 'woman',
    for she was taken out of man."

²⁴For this reason a man will leave his father and mother and be united to his wife, and they will become one flesh.

²⁵The man and his wife were both naked, and they felt no shame.

The Fall

3 Now the serpent was more crafty than any of the wild animals the Lord God had made. He said to the woman, "Did God really say, 'You must not eat from any tree in the garden'?"

²The woman said to the serpent, "We may eat fruit from the trees in the garden, ³but God did say, 'You must not eat fruit from the tree that is in the middle of the garden, and you must not touch it, or you will die.' "

⁴"You will not surely die," the serpent said to the woman. ⁵"For God knows that when you eat of it your eyes will be opened, and you will be like God, knowing good and evil."

⁶When the woman saw that the fruit of the tree was good for food and pleasing to the eye, and also desirable for gaining wisdom, she took some and ate it. She also gave some to her husband, who was with her, and he ate it. ⁷Then the eyes of both

of them were opened, and they realised that they were naked; so they sewed fig leaves together and made coverings for themselves.

⁸Then the man and his wife heard the sound of the Lord God as he was walking in the garden in the cool of the day, and they hid from the Lord God among the trees of the garden. ⁹But the Lord God called to the man, "Where are you?"

¹⁰He answered, "I heard you in the garden, and I was afraid because I was naked; so I hid."

¹¹And he said, "Who told you that you were naked: Have you eaten from the tree from which I commanded you not to eat?"

¹²The man said, "The woman you put here with me—she gave me some fruit from the tree, and I ate it."

¹³Then the Lord God said to the woman, "What is this you have done?"

The woman said, "The serpent deceived me, and I ate it."

¹⁴So the Lord God said to the serpent, "Because you have done this,

"Cursed are you above all the
    livestock
    and all the wild animals!
You will crawl on your belly
    and you will eat dust
    all the days of your life.
¹⁵And I will put enmity
    between you and the woman,
    and between your offspring and
    hers;
he will crush your head
    and you will strike his heel."

Loneliness is in essence a homesickness for God. It is a feeling of not counting, not mattering to anyone and not being significant. Glenda Jackson said, 'It is very lonely being a human being – even when you are in a crowd.' Thomas Wolf, the novelist and playwright said that loneliness is the 'central and inevitable fact of human existence'. Mother Teresa said, 'The greatest disease today is not starvation but loneliness.' What is the cause of this loneliness?

Although this passage comes very early in the Bible, we already come across Satan or the devil, seen in this account as a serpent. This image rightly reveals that the devil is both crafty and poisonous. He is real and he is the main opponent of God and of Christian people. Here we see how he tries to change our lives for the worse.

First God gives a wide-ranging **permission**: 'You are free to eat from any tree in the garden' (2:16). There is one **prohibition**: 'but you must not eat from the tree of the knowledge of good and evil' (17) and God warns of the **penalty**, 'for when you eat of it you will surely die'. In the following verses we see Satan's tactics.

STEP 1 – SATAN IGNORES THE PERMISSION (V. 1)
Adam and Eve have been given permission by God to eat from any tree in the luscious garden of Eden, except one. Satan ignores the far-reaching and liberal permission.

STEP 2 – HE CONCENTRATES ON THE PROHIBITION (V. 1)

Satan concentrates on the one prohibition, that they should not eat from the tree of the knowledge of good and evil. Even then he exaggerates, saying that God has banned the fruit of all the trees (v. 1). Satan is still the same today. Who do you think upholds the image of Christianity as a restrictive list of rules? He conveniently forgets to portray the enjoyment of knowing Jesus: the peace and freedom, the love and joy.

STEP 3 – HE DENIES THE PENALTY (V. 4)

Finally, Satan denies the penalty of disobeying God. By saying, 'You will not surely die' (v. 4), he is suggesting that Adam and Eve will come to no harm if they go against God.

It is a big lie and an effective one. Tragically, our society is living under that lie. It is easy to think that we are missing out on something good if we obey God, but the opposite is true. It is disobedience which causes us to miss out on so much of what God has intended for us, and it is disobedience which ultimately leads us to ruin.

In the verses that follow we see the consequences. They are psychological, theological and social.

1. Psychological (v. 7)

Sin affects us by causing an alienation within ourselves. Adam and Eve 'sewed fig leaves together and made coverings for themselves'. After their sin, they felt shame and embarrassment about being themselves. Having gone astray from God, they were ill at ease within themselves. So often we wear masks to hide our true selves.

2. Theological (v. 10)

Sin affects our relationship with God as we become alienated from him. Adam and Eve hid from the Lord God. They were living in God's world without a relationship with him. That is why loneliness is a homesickness for God. There is within every human being what is often referred to as 'a God-shaped gap'.

3. Social (vv. 12–13)

Sin affects our relationships with others and we experience an alienation from our fellow human beings. Adam blamed Eve, Eve blamed the serpent, and the breakdown in human relationships began. We see the continuation of this now in the breakdown of marriages, family life, community life and on an international scale in war.

Right from the start God is looking to restore the relationship. He calls out, 'Where are you?' (v. 9). There is a hint of the ultimate resolution in verse 15: 'he [Jesus] will crush your [Satan's] head and you [Satan] will strike his [Jesus'] heel'. Jesus was nailed to a cross without even a fig leaf to cover him. He was cut off from God and cut off from his friends for us. It is here that we find the answer to our loneliness. As Frank Colquhoun, Anglican author and theologian, said, 'When Christ saves a person, he saves them not only from their sin, he also saves them from their solitude.'

Once we have entered a relationship with God, our solitude is over. For every person who puts their faith in Christ will one day see him face to face and be with him eternally. Even now, by his Spirit he is always beside us. As you go through the day remember he is with you always.

🖐 PRAY

You might like to pray the prayer of the psalmist:

Be my shepherd throughout the whole of my life, and when '... I walk through the valley of the shadow of death, I will fear no evil, for you are with me' (Psalm 23).

WHAT HAPPENS WHEN WE DIE?

1 THESSALONIANS 4:13 – 5:11

The Lord will punish those who commit such sins, as we have already told you and warned you. ²For God did not call us to be impure, but to live a holy life. ³Therefore, he who rejects this instruction does not reject mere human beings but God, who gives you his Holy Spirit.

⁹Now about your mutual love we do not need to write to you, for you yourselves have been taught by God to love each other. ¹⁰And in fact, you do love all the brothers and sisters throughout Macedonia. Yet we urge you, dear friends, to do so more and more.

¹¹Make it your ambition to lead a quiet life, to mind your own business and to work with your hands, just as we told you, ¹²so that your daily life may win the respect of outsiders and so that you will not be dependent on anybody.

The Coming of the LORD

¹³Brothers and sisters, we do not want you to be ignorant about those who fall asleep, or to grieve like the rest, who have no hope. ¹⁴We believe that Jesus died and rose again and so we believe that God will bring with Jesus those who have fallen asleep in him. ¹⁵According to the Lord's own word, we tell you that we who are still alive, who are left till the coming of the Lord, will certainly not precede those who have fallen asleep. ¹⁶For the Lord himself will come down from heaven, with a loud command, with the voice of the archangel and with the trumpet call of God, and the dead in Christ will rise first. ¹⁷After that, we who are still alive and are left will be caught up together with them in the clouds to meet the Lord in the air. And so we

will be with the Lord for ever. ¹⁸Therefore encourage each other with these words.

5 Now, brothers and sisters, about times and dates we do not need to write to you, ²for you know very well that the day of the Lord will come like a thief in the night. ³While people are saying, "Peace and safety", destruction will come on them suddenly, as labour pains on a pregnant woman, and they will not escape.

⁴But you, brothers and sisters, are not in darkness so that this day should surprise you like a thief. ⁵You are all children of the light and children of the day. We do not belong to the night or to the darkness. ⁶So then, let us not be like others, who are asleep, but let us be alert and self-controlled. ⁷For those who sleep, sleep at night, and those who get drunk, get drunk at night. ⁸But since we belong to the day, let us be self-controlled, putting on faith and love as a breastplate, and the hope of salvation as a helmet. ⁹For God did not appoint us to suffer wrath but to receive salvation through our Lord Jesus Christ. ¹⁰He died for us so that, whether we are awake or asleep, we may live together with him. ¹¹Therefore encourage one another and build each other up, just as in fact you are doing.

Final Instructions

¹²Now we ask you, brothers and sisters, to respect those who work hard among you, who are over you in the Lord and who admonish you. ¹³Hold them in the highest regard in love because of their work. Live in peace with each other. ¹⁴And we urge you, brothers and sisters, to respect those who work hard among you,

The late Canon David Watson who died of cancer at the age of fifty-one said, 'No one can live well until he can die well.' Paul wrote this letter to Christian people who were worried about death. They were worried about their relatives and friends who had died and also presumably about themselves. What happens to them and us when we die?

So many people would say that no one knows the answers to these questions but Paul writes, 'We do not want you to be ignorant' (4:13). We can find out the answers. Our hope lies in the return of Jesus Christ. There are over 300 references to the second coming in the New Testament. This is not 'pie in the sky when you die' but rather the centre of our Christian hope, and it is fundamental to our thinking. It involves:

1. A UNIQUE HOPE (4:13)
Christians have a unique hope. Paul writes, 'We do not want you... to grieve like the rest, who have no hope' (4:13). It is not wrong to grieve. Grief is important, and we should not suppress it, but the grief of the Christian is (totally) unlike that experienced by those who have no hope. It has been said that 'Other people see only a hopeless end, but the Christian rejoices in an endless hope.'

2. A CERTAIN FUTURE (4:14)
Hope in the Christian sense is no mere human wishful thinking. It is not a pious hope, theoretical or speculative. It is not based on emotion, nor is it a crutch. It is built on historical events (4:14). Jesus removed the sting of death on the cross as he bore the full horror of death on our behalf. We don't have to face what he has already faced for us. So Paul speaks of death as falling asleep and falling asleep (if you're anything like me) is something to look forward to. We need not dread death because the next thing we will experience is waking up, and waking up in the presence of God and all who have died in faith. Jesus rose

again and demonstrated conclusively that death is conquered. The resurrection is the guarantee of Christian hope. This total certainty is not arrogant because it is based not on anything we've done or will do but on what Jesus did and said.

3. A GLORIOUS ETERNITY (4:16–17)
We will be 'with the Lord forever', which is the Christian's idea of bliss. There will be no illness, no crying or pain but only pure joy. This gives a new perspective to this life with all its trials, temptations and disappointments. We shall never again be parted from the Lord or from those we love. We will be caught up 'together with them' (4:17). There will be a great reunion in heaven. Paul writes, 'Therefore, encourage each other with these words' (4:18).

4. A SUDDEN JUDGMENT (5:1–3)
Various groups have tried to predict the timing of the Lord's return. But Jesus, Peter, John and Paul all tell us that he will come back 'like a thief in the night' (5:5). We don't know when this will be. But we do know that he will return. The point is that we must always be ready.

"we really feel that the Lord will arrive so— after lunch on Tuesday, —assuming Marjorie's finished her ballet lesson"

There is a warning in this passage for those who reject Jesus. There is a dark side of our hope.

Paul speaks of 'destruction' (v. 3), no escape (v. 3) and 'wrath' (v. 9). These are solemn and serious words. But he writes to assure the Thessalonians that they have nothing to fear: 'but you are not in darkness' (5:4). He assures them that they will not 'suffer wrath' but will 'receive salvation through our Lord Jesus Christ' (v. 9).

5. A TRANSFORMED LIFE (5:4–11)

Not only do we have a unique hope, a certain future and a glorious eternity but we are enjoying a foretaste of it now. We are 'children of the light and children of the day' (5:5) because God has already broken into history. There is life before death as well as after death: Jesus 'died for us so that whether we are awake or asleep we may live together with him' (v. 10).

We are already enjoying the relationship with God which is eternal life. Yet we cannot simply sit back and enjoy it. If we are aware that others are missing out now and will miss out even more in the future, we must do all we can now to give others hope. As David Watson put it, 'Christ wants disciples who not only have hope but also give hope.'

💧 PRAY

Thank God today for the hope he gives us.
Thank him that he has given us all a secure future, that we can look forward to a glorious eternity with the Lord and with all those we love who have died in Christ.
Thank him for rescuing you from the coming judgment. Pray for his help to live a new life, 'alert and self-controlled' (5:6), putting on faith and love as a breastplate, and the hope of salvation as a helmet' (5:8).

GOING THROUGH HARD TIMES
2 CORINTHIANS 1:3–11

2 CORINTHIANS

1 Paul, an apostle of Christ Jesus by the will of God, and Timothy our brother,

To the church of God in Corinth, together with all the saints throughout Achaia:

²Grace and peace to you from God our Father and the Lord Jesus Christ.

The God of All Comfort

³Praise be to the God and Father of our Lord Jesus Christ, the Father of compassion and the God of all comfort, ⁴who comforts us in all our troubles, so that we can comfort those in any trouble with the comfort we ourselves have received from God. ⁵For just as the sufferings of Christ flow over into our lives, so also through Christ our comfort overflows. ⁶If we are distressed, it is for your comfort and salvation; if we are comforted, it is for your comfort, which produces in you patient endurance of the same sufferings we suffer. ⁷And our hope for you is firm, because we know that just as you share in our sufferings, so also you share in our comfort.

⁸We do not want you to be uninformed, brothers and sisters, about the hardships we suffered in the province of Asia. We were under great pressure, far beyond our ability to endure, so that we despaired even of life. ⁹Indeed, in our hearts we felt the sentence of death. But this happened that we might not rely on ourselves but on God, who raises the dead. ¹⁰He has delivered us from such a deadly peril, and he will deliver us. On him we have set our hope that he will continue to deliver us, ¹¹as you help us by your prayers. Then many will give thanks on our behalf for the gracious favour granted us in answer to the prayers of many.

Paul's Change of Plans

¹²Now this is our boast: Our conscience testifies that we have conducted ourselves in the world, and especially in our relations with you, in the holiness and sincerity that are from God. We have done so not according to worldly wisdom but according to God's grace. ¹³For we do not write to you anything you cannot read or understand. And I hope that, ¹⁴as you have understood us in part, you will come to understand fully that you can boast of us just as we will boast of you in the day of the Lord Jesus.

¹⁵Because I was confident of this, I planned to visit you first so that you might benefit twice. ¹⁶I planned to visit you on my way to Macedonia and to come back to you from Macedonia, and then to have you send me on my way to Judea. ¹⁷When I planned this, did I do it lightly? Or do I make my plans in a worldly manner so that in the same breath I say, "Yes, yes" and "No, no"?

¹⁸But as surely as God is faithful, our message to you is not "Yes" and "No." ¹⁹For the Son of God, Jesus Christ, who was preached among you by me and Silas and Timothy, was not "Yes" and "No," but in

We all go through times when things go wrong. We may have experienced hard times: bereavement, rejection, injustice, disappointments, unemployment, financial problems or relationships going wrong. Why does God allow it? Are there any benefits?

This is the most personal letter Paul wrote. He reveals his feelings as a man of flesh and blood. He knows what it is to be hurt and depressed. He speaks of troubles (v. 4), sufferings (vv. 5–8), distress (v. 6), hardships (v. 8), pressure (v. 8), despair (v. 8), sentence of death (v. 9) and deadly peril (v. 10).

Paul knew about persecution. He had been imprisoned, chained with three feet of chain to a Roman soldier. He had been flogged five times with thirty-nine lashes. He had been beaten three times with rods. Once he had been stoned. He knew about hardship – lack of sleep, hunger and thirst. He knew what it was to be cold and naked. He had suffered fatigue and exhaustion. He knew about pressure. He had experienced temptation, sickness and all the trials of life (2 Corinthians 6:4–10; 11:23–29).

This is not a philosophical or even theological discussion of why God allows suffering. He starts with praise. He is not praising God for the suffering nor seeking it. Instead, in spite of it, he is praising God for the positive benefits which have come out of it. He speaks of seven blessings.

"he didn't have to endure tambourines."

1. THE BLESSING OF THE PRESENCE OF GOD (V. 4)

The Greek word for comfort (vv. 4–7) means to encourage, cheer or come alongside. Trouble and persecution can either drive us away from God or closer to him. God is the 'Father of compassion and God of all comfort'. As we draw close to him, we find that he does care and that he suffers with us.

2. THE BLESSING OF BEING ABLE TO COMFORT OTHERS (V. 4)

Those who have suffered themselves are usually the best equipped to help others in their suffering. When we have a tough time, we often become more compassionate and more willing to empathise, support and help rather than criticise or judge.

3. THE BLESSING OF CHRISTIAN CHARACTER (V. 6)

Suffering produces 'patient endurance'. The Greek word means patience, endurance, fortitude, steadfastness and perseverance. As gold is refined by fire and as the pruning of the vine produces fruit, so we become purer and more effective as we experience difficulty.

Oscar Wilde wrote, 'Now it seems to me that love of some kind is the only possible explanation for the extraordinary amount of suffering that there is in the world… because in no other way could the soul of man, for whom the world was made, reach the full stature of its perfection' (*De Profundis*, Penguin Classics, 1973, p. 162).

4. THE BLESSING OF CHRISTIAN FRIENDSHIP (V. 7)

The Greek word for 'share' refers to partnership. We are all partners in Christ, part of the same body. If localised physical pain affects one's whole body, it follows that the suffering of one person in the body of Christ will bring pain to all. Conversely, the joy of one person will cause all to rejoice. Ultimately, these shared experiences enrich our lives and teach us how to be a true community.

5. THE BLESSING OF LEARNING TO TRUST GOD (VV. 8–9)

When we are in a time of prosperity, we risk becoming independent or proud and may even start to trust ourselves more than God. But, when everything goes wrong and we have reached the end of our own resources there is nothing more we can do. We are thrown into true dependence on God. God's strength is made perfect in weakness (2 Corinthians 12:10).

6. THE BLESSING OF SEEING GOD'S DELIVERANCE (V. 10)

Paul speaks of the three tenses of God's deliverance: past, present and future. We are free from the despair of the past, free from any fear of the future and able to face the present with faith in God.

7. THE BLESSING OF ANSWERED PRAYER (V. 11)

Problems often lead to prayer and prayer often leads to solutions. This in turn leads to God being thanked.

'He has delivered us... he will deliver us. On him we have set our hope...' (v.10). Today, you could thank God for all the ways he has delivered you in the past. Bring to God all the major challenges and problems you face in the weeks and months ahead. Commit them into his hands and set your hope on him.

'As you help us by your prayers' (v.11). Your prayers make a difference. Pray for those you know who are going through hard times at the moment – that 'many will give thanks' for the 'gracious favour granted... in answer to the prayers of many' (v.11).

✋ PRAY

You may like to pray the prayer of Corrie ten Boom:

'Thank you, Lord Jesus that you will be our hiding place, whatever happens.'

A PARADIGM SHIFT

COLOSSIANS 3:1-17

false humility and the worship of angels disqualify you for the prize. Such a person goes into great detail about what he has seen, and his unspiritual mind puffs him up with idle notions. ¹⁹He has lost connection with the Head, from whom the whole body, supported and held together by its ligaments and sinews, grows as God causes it to grow.

²⁰Since you died with Christ to the basic principles of this world, why, as though you still belonged to it, do you submit to its rules: ²¹"Do not handle! Do not taste! Do not touch!"? ²²These are all destined to perish with use, because they are based on human commands and teachings. ²³Such regulations indeed have an appearance of wisdom, with their self-imposed worship, their false humility and their harsh treatment of the body, but they lack any value in restraining sensual indulgence.

Rules for Holy Living

3 Since, then, you have been raised with Christ, set your hearts on things above, where Christ is seated at the right hand of God. ²Set your minds on things above, not on earthly things. ³For you died, and your life is now hidden with Christ in God. ⁴When Christ, who is your life, appears, then you also will appear with him in glory.

⁵Put to death, therefore, whatever belongs to your earthly nature: sexual immorality, impurity, lust, evil desires and greed, which is idolatry. ⁶Because of these, the wrath of God is coming. ⁷You used to walk in these ways, in the life you once lived. ⁸But now you must rid yourselves of all such things as

these: anger, rage, malice, slander and filthy language from your lips. ⁹Do not lie to each other, since you have taken off your old self with its practices ¹⁰and have put on the new self, which is being renewed in knowledge in the image of its Creator. ¹¹Here there is no Greek or Jew, circumcised or uncircumcised, barbarian, Scythian, slave or free, but Christ is all, and is in all.

¹²Therefore, as God's chosen people, holy and dearly loved, clothe yourselves with compassion, kindness, humility, gentleness and patience. ¹³Bear with each other and forgive whatever grievances you may have against one another. Forgive as the Lord forgave you. ¹⁴And over all these virtues put on love, which binds them all together in perfect unity.

¹⁵Let the peace of Christ rule in your hearts, since as members of one body you were called to peace. And be thankful. ¹⁶Let the word of Christ dwell in you richly as you teach and admonish one another with all wisdom, and as you sing psalms, hymns and spiritual songs with gratitude in your hearts to God. ¹⁷And whatever you do, whether in word or deed, do it all in the name of the Lord Jesus, giving thanks to God the father through him.

Rules for Christian Households

¹⁸Wives, submit to your husbands, as is fitting in the Lord.

¹⁹Husbands, love your wives and do not be harsh with them.

²⁰Children, obey your parents in everything, for this pleases the Lord.

²¹Fathers, do not embitter your children, or they will become discouraged.

The term 'paradigm shift' was introduced by the philosopher of science, Thomas Kuhn. He showed how almost every significant breakthrough in the field of scientific endeavour is first a break with tradition, the old ways of thinking and the old paradigms. Copernicus created a paradigm shift by seeing the sun, rather than the earth, as the centre of the universe. Suddenly everything took on a different interpretation.

"The Sun? Copernicus, your stomach's the centre of the universe"

The apostle Paul encourages his readers to make a 'paradigm shift'. A relationship with God through Jesus Christ affects who we are and all our relationships. We should see everything in a new light.

Many of Paul's letters can be divided into two distinct parts. In this one the first part is to do with doctrine (the nature of Christ and the gospel). The second part is concerned with the practical outworking of becoming a Christian. What we believe affects how we live, which is why what we believe matters so much. Paul writes here that being a Christian will make us different from other people. How does this paradigm shift affect our lives?

1. CHANGE IN OURSELVES (VV. 1–12)

There are many self-help books and much success literature that teach techniques to sort ourselves and our lives out and offer us superficial solutions. But what matters most is much more fundamental: our characters.

We died with Christ, were raised with him and we will one day appear with him (vv. 1–4). The old self has died so that we are to get rid of the old ways and live in the power and presence of God. Paul uses an image of changing our clothes: we are to take off old habits and put on new ones.

Take off the old clothes

First, the old clothing may involve the misuse of sex and money (vv. 5-6). There is nothing wrong with these things in themselves except insofar as they are misused and become idols (v. 5). When this happens, serious consequences follow (v. 6). Second, our old clothing may include sins of speech: using language aggressively and destructively (vv. 8–9). Third, it may include discrimination (v. 11). Among Christians there should be no racial, religious or class barriers. We are all God's chosen people, holy and loved by him (v. 12).

We are to put on the new clothes

The new clothes offer us an alternative way of behaving and responding to each other: compassion rather than malice, kindness rather than slander, humility rather than anger, gentleness rather than rage and patience rather than bad language.

2. CHANGE IN OUR RELATIONSHIPS WITH OTHERS (VV. 13–15)
Forgiveness (v. 13)

Forgiveness is a uniquely Christian virtue. Others may forgive but only Christians have a real basis for it. We have to forgive because we have experienced God's forgiveness. We will never forgive to the extent that we have been forgiven.

Love (v. 14)
This is not just an emotion but something we are to 'put on' and which binds everything else together.

Peace (v. 15)
The kind of peace that Paul speaks about here is only possible when the peace of Christ is filling our hearts.

3. CHANGE IN OUR ATTITUDE TO JESUS (VV. 16–17)
Listening to him (v. 16a)
We experience a longing to hear Jesus and a thirst for the word of God. Our priorities change, and we find time to study the Bible regularly, meditating on it and putting it into practice.

Worshipping him (v. 16b)
We respond to God's love for us by expressing our love and thankfulness to him in worship – 'as you sing psalms, hymns and spiritual songs with gratitude in your hearts to God'.

Centring our lives on him (v. 17)
Whatever we do, whether in word or deed, we should do it all in the name of the Lord Jesus. Our families, our jobs, our friends, money, possessions and leisure activities are all important and have their place but none of them should be at the centre of our lives. That place should be reserved for Jesus and him alone.

We can change. Jesus died to make it possible for us to live a new life. We must change and as we move on in our life with Jesus, we will change. We will be transformed into his likeness.

🖐 PRAY

O Lord, fill me with the grace of Jesus so that increasingly his beauty may be seen in me.

WHERE DO I FIT IN?

ACTS 2:42-47

nor did his body see decay. God has raised this Jesus to life, and we are all witnesses of the fact. Exalted to the right hand of God, he has received from the Father the promised Holy Spirit and has poured out what you now see and hear. For David did not ascend to heaven, and yet he said,

" 'The Lord said to my Lord:
"Sit at my right hand
until I make your enemies
a footstool for your feet." '

"Therefore let all Israel be assured of this: God has made this Jesus, whom you crucified, both Lord and Christ."

When the people heard this, they were cut to the heart and said to Peter and the other apostles, "Brothers, what shall we do?"

Peter replied, "Repent and be baptised, every one of you, in the name of Jesus Christ for the forgiveness of your sins. And you will receive the gift of the Holy Spirit. The promise is for you and your children and for all who are far off—for all whom the Lord our God will call."

With many other words he warned them; and he pleaded with them, "Save yourselves from this corrupt generation." Those who accepted his message were baptised, and about three thousand were added to their number that day.

The Fellowship of the Believers

They devoted themselves to the apostles' teaching and to the fellowship, to the breaking of bread and to prayer. Everyone was filled with awe, and many wonders and miraculous signs were done by the apostles. All the believers were together and had everything in common. Selling their possessions and goods, they gave to anyone who had need. Every day they continued to meet together in the temple courts. They broke bread in their homes and ate together with glad and sincere hearts, praising God and enjoying the favour of all the people. And the Lord added to their number daily those who were being saved.

Peter Heals the Crippled Beggar

One day Peter and John were going up to the temple at the time of prayer—at three in the afternoon. Now a man crippled from birth was being carried to the temple gate called Beautiful, where he was put every day to beg from those going into the temple courts. When he saw Peter and John about to enter, he asked them for money. Peter looked straight at him, as did John. Then Peter said, "Look at us!" So the man gave them his attention, expecting to get something from them.

Then Peter said, "Silver or gold I do not have, but what I have I give you. In the name of Jesus Christ of Nazareth, walk." Taking him by the right hand, he helped him up, and instantly the man's feet and ankles became strong. He jumped to his feet and began to walk. Then he went with them into the temple courts, walking and jumping, and praising God. When all the people saw him walking and praising God, they recognised him as the same man who used to sit begging at the temple gate called Beautiful, and they were filled with wonder and amazement at what had happened to him.

Katherine, a Mennonite woman aged forty, had been sent to a labour farm in Siberia because of her Christian faith. She lived in appalling conditions with no heating, only a board with some straw on it for her bed and inadequate blankets for warmth.

Her relatives in Canada had for several years tried to get permission from the Russian government for Katherine to come and visit them. Finally permission was granted. When Katherine arrived in Vancouver she couldn't imagine that people could live with so many possessions. She went from relative to relative, staying in their beautiful homes full of beautiful things and was treated royally.

They planned that she should defect, find work and be cared for by her relatives. But Katherine wanted to go home. She said, 'I don't think I can explain to you why it is I want to go back. All I can say is that over here in this country, you people have your things and you are busy all day long. Over there we don't have anything, but we have each other. I want to get back to my brothers and sisters in Christ where we live for one another.'

These verses in Acts describe the church just after it had

"Maybe if we had taken her skiing or something."

swelled to over 3,000 people in its first day of existence! Exciting things happen when the people of God get together to celebrate. We see that in the great festivals of the Old Testament and we see it again around the world today. At this festival of Pentecost people had experienced the visible, audible presence of God (Acts 2:1–4). There must have been an incredible sense of worship and awe. But awe-inspiring times of celebration where hundreds or thousands of people gather to worship may simultaneously inspire us and make us feel lonely.

Such experiences may lead us to ask: 'Where do I fit in?' 'How can I make friends?' 'How can I contribute?' 'How can I grow in my faith?' 'How can I be more effective?' or 'What can I do?' The answers were found in the groups of Christians which gathered in homes after Pentecost. They were led by ordinary people (Acts 18:1–3; Romans 16:3–5; 1 Corinthians 16:19), men and women doing ordinary jobs. Similar groups exist today, and are at the heart of church life.

On the day of Pentecost the disciples had experienced the love of God being poured into their hearts by the Holy Spirit (Romans 5:5). Now this love overflowed in three directions.

1. THEY LOVED GOD
Teaching (v. 42a)
'They devoted themselves to the apostles' teaching.' They wanted to know what God was saying to them. This 'teaching' can now be found in the New Testament. Through the Bible, God speaks to us and we get to know Jesus Christ better. Home groups are an ideal place to study the Bible together.

Prayer (v. 42b)
Their prayer meetings were never dull. They were times of great excitement. Again, home groups are the ideal place to pray for one another, especially if we are going through difficult times. We can

also unite in small groups to pray for specific issues, individuals, or for our country.

Food (v. 42)
They had a meal together and in the 'breaking of bread' they remembered Jesus' presence and death for them.

Worship (v. 47)
They praised God together. We should expect to meet God intimately through worship. This is the highest and most fulfilling calling that we can know. Our main purpose in life is 'to glorify God and enjoy him forever' (*Westminster Catechism*).

2. THEY LOVED ONE ANOTHER
Erich Fromm writes in his book *The Sane Society*, 'There is not much love to be found in the world of our day. There is rather a superficial friendliness concealing a distance, an indifference, a subtle distrust' (Holt Paperbacks, 1990, p. 139). In a world characterised by loneliness, alienation and individualism, there is a greater need than ever to belong. The church of Jesus Christ and in particular the small group is the place to find Christian friendship and fellowship.

Home groups are places to love and be loved, to encourage and be encouraged. The atmosphere should be open, non-judgmental and honest enough to allow friendships to deepen (see Romans 16:3-4). It should be a group of people who stick with one another through thick and thin. We should know we can rely on one another and trust each other totally.

They demonstrated love
These early Christians did not just feel love but they loved one another practically and actively on a daily basis. It has been said that if Christians were for one day what they ought to be, the world

would be converted overnight.

They supported one another
There was a radical generosity of spirit which was entirely voluntary (Acts 4:34). They renounced possessiveness and shared their resources. Generosity takes many forms: giving financially to one another, sharing our possessions and making time for one another, offering hospitality and practical help.

They used their gifts
Each person contributed their gifts: teaching, hospitality, giving or leading worship. The small group is the place where we discover where we fit in. We minister to one another as parts of the body of Christ and find that our different gifts complement each other.

They had fun together
'They ate together with glad and sincere hearts' (v. 46). A gloomy Christian is a contradiction in terms. A home group should be, among other things, a place of laughter and enjoyment.

3. THEY LOVED THE WORLD
They went out into the world with wonders and miraculous signs (v. 43). They were respected by everyone and the Lord added to their number (v. 47). They looked outwards. If small groups look inwards they will stagnate and die. If they are looking out they will have the joy of seeing other people's lives changed, the same sort of joy that parents have watching their children growing up.

The small group is not always easy because all of us can be difficult to help and difficult to love. However, we are changed by shared experience and, within the highs and lows of such a group, we discover the joy of true relationship (eg see Apollos – Acts 18:24; 1 Corinthians 1:12; 3:4-6; 4:6; Titus 3:13).

This is the church at its most vibrant and attractive. It is vital to be an active participant in a church which encourages you in your faith and gives you an opportunity to serve God. We cannot do it on our own.

🖐 PRAY

If you do not already belong to such a group, pray that God will guide you and then seek out such a gathering.

'HOW MY LIFE WAS CHANGED'

ISAIAH 6:1-8

[27]Not one of them grows tired or
stumbles,
not one slumbers or sleeps;
not a belt is loosened at the waist,
not a sandal thong is broken.
[28]Their arrows are sharp,
all their bows are strung;
their horses' hoofs seem like
flint,
their chariot wheels like a
whirlwind.
[29]Their roar is like that of the lion,
they roar like young lions;
they growl as they seize their prey
and carry it off with no-one to
rescue.
[30]In that day they will roar over it
like the roaring of the sea.
And if one looks at the land,
there is only darkness and
distress;
even the light will be darkened
by the clouds.

Isaiah's Commission

6 In the year that King Uzziah died, I saw the Lord seated on a throne, high and exalted, and the train of his robe filled the temple. [2]Above him were seraphs, each with six wings: With two wings they covered their faces, with two they covered their feet, and with two they were flying. [3]And they were calling to one another:

"Holy, holy, holy is the Lord
Almighty;
the whole earth is full of his
glory."

[4]At the sound of their voices the doorposts and thresholds shook and the temple was filled with smoke.
[5]"Woe to me!" I cried. "I am ruined! For I am a man of unclean lips, and I live among a people of unclean lips, and my eyes have seen the King, the Lord Almighty."
[6]Then one of the seraphs flew to me with a live coal in his hand, which he had taken with tongs from the altar. [7]With it he touched my mouth and said, "See, this has touched your lips; your guilt is taken away and your sin atoned for."
[8]Then I heard the voice of the Lord saying, "Whom shall I send? And who will go for us?"
And I said, "Here am I. Send me!"
[9]He said, "Go and tell this people:

" 'Be ever hearing, but never
understanding;
be ever seeing, but never
perceiving.'
[10]Make the heart of this people
calloused;
make their ears dull
and close their eyes.
Otherwise they might see with
their eyes,
hear with their ears,
understand with their hearts,
and turn and be healed."

[11]Then I said, "For how long, O
Lord?"
And he answered:

"Until the cities lie ruined
and without inhabitant,
until the houses are left deserted
and the fields ruined and
ravaged
[12]until the Lord has sent

There is great power in a testimony. In this passage the prophet Isaiah speaks about how God turned his life around in about 736 BC. God revealed to him what was going on around him, and Isaiah describes the state of affairs in Israel in the first five chapters of the book of Isaiah. The people had turned their backs on God (1:4). There was corruption (1:4), formality in religion (1:11), materialism, arrogance, godlessness, drunkenness and carousing (5:20–27). God called him to do something about it by speaking out to his generation. How did this happen?

1. HE CAUGHT A GLIMPSE OF WHO GOD REALLY IS (VV. 1–4)
Isaiah tries to describe what he has seen of the majesty, holiness, glory and power of God in language which we may find difficult to relate to. He is using his own words to describe a powerful encounter with the living God.

2. HE FELT TOTALLY UNWORTHY AND INADEQUATE FOR THE TASK (V. 5)
When he saw the holiness of God he said, 'Woe to me! I am ruined!' Our sense of sin is related to how close we are to God. The closer we are to the light the more we are aware of the dirt. First, he is aware of his own sin. He says, 'I am a man of unclean lips.' Second, he realises that he lives among a people of unclean lips, surrounded by sin. We pick up dirt as we walk through the world. We cannot avoid it.

Isaiah has a sense of his own unworthiness and inadequacy. God breaks our hearts as he shows us what we are like. Oscar Wilde wrote: 'A man's very highest moment is, I have no doubt at all, when he kneels in the dust, and beats his breast, and tells all the sins of his life' (*De Profundis*, Penguin Classics, p. 197).

But God does not leave us there...

3. HE EXPERIENCES THE MERCY OF GOD (V. 6)

Our guilt would destroy us but God took the initiative and provided the means of our cleansing. He took away Isaiah's guilt and atoned for his sin. Now we understand that this was possible through the cross of Jesus Christ. We all have the opportunity to experience his forgiveness and his love. In spite of all we have done, God loves us.

The experience of our own sin is the answer to pride. The experience of the love of God is the answer to insecurity. Both were dealt with at the cross. Without him we can do nothing (John 15:5). 'I can do everything through him...' (Philippians 4:13).

The past is dealt with. We do not need to go around loaded with guilt but rather filled with the knowledge of God's love for us.

4. HE RESPONDED TO GOD'S CALL (V. 8)

God asked him the question: 'I have done all this for you – now will you go for me?' His whole life was before him. What was he going to do with it? His response was to surrender his will. He said, 'Here am I. Send me!' (v. 8). He did not make any excuses. He didn't say, 'I am too busy.' He didn't offer to do it later, or when he was less tired or had sorted out some problem.

It was an unconditional response. He didn't say, 'Send me, I am going that way anyhow' or 'Send me, I was planning to do that' or 'Send me, I rather like the sound of that idea.' He said, 'Send me to do anything you want, Lord.' That is true commitment and true service. Isaiah gave God a straight 'yes'. We need to do the same. We will never have a better opportunity than now.

Isaiah was willing to be used as a servant and God sent him to speak to the entire nation. When we say to God, 'Here I am. Send me!' he will use us as his servant. This may well be in our place of work, with our family or with our neighbours and friends. In due course, it may even be further afield. In that case he will give us clear guidance.

We, unlike Isaiah, are living in the age of the Spirit when the Holy Spirit has come to live in every Christian. If God wanted to do this for Isaiah, how much more will he do it for you?

✋ PRAY

Have you caught a glimpse of God? Ask God to reveal himself to you: his majesty, holiness, glory and power. When we catch a glimpse of God, we feel compelled to confess our own unworthiness and ask him for his mercy. Then we can offer ourselves to his service by saying, 'Here I am. Send me.'

ALPHA TITLES AVAILABLE

Why Jesus?
A booklet –given to all participants at the start of the Alpha course. 'The clearest, best illustrated and most challenging short presentation of Jesus that I know.' – Michael Green

Why Christmas?
The Christmas version of *Why Jesus?*

Questions of Life
The Alpha course in book form. In fifteen compelling chapters Nicky Gumbel points the way to an authentic Christianity that is exciting and relevant to today's world.

Searching Issues
The seven issues most often raised by participants on the Alpha course: suffering, other religions, sex before marriage, the New Age, homosexuality, science and Christianity, and the Trinity.

A Life Worth Living
What happens after Alpha? Based on the book of Philippians, this is an invaluable next step for those who have just completed the Alpha course, and for anyone eager to put their faith on a firm biblical footing.

The Jesus Lifestyle
Studies on the Sermon on the Mount showing how Jesus' teaching flies in the face of a modern lifestyle and presents us with a radical alternative.

All titles are by Nicky Gumbel, who is Vicar of HTB

To order www.alpharesources.org

If you are interested in finding out more about Alpha please contact:

Alpha U.S.A.
2275 Half Day Road
Suite 185
Deerfield, IL 60015
Tel: 800.362.5742
Tel: + 212.406.5269
e-mail: info@alphausa.org
www.alphausa.org
www.alpharesources.org

Alpha in the Caribbean
Alpha Office Chagunas
1 Rene Street
Chagunas, Trinidad W.I.
Face Book: AlphaInTheCaribbean
Twitter: @AlphaCaribbean

Alpha Canada
Suite #230 – 11331 Coppersmith Way
Richmond, BC V7A 5J9
Tel: 800.743.0899
Fax: 604.271.6124
e-mail: office@alphacanada.org
www.alphacanada.org

To purchase resources in Canada:

David C. Cook Distribution
Canada
P.O. Box 98, 55 Woodslee Avenue
Paris, ON N3L 3E5
Tel: 800.263.2664
Fax: 800.461.8575
e-mail: custserve@davidccook.ca
www.davidccook.ca

CPSIA information can be obtained at www.ICGtesting.com
Printed in the USA
BVOW03s1825051214

377053BV00001B/1/P

9 781938 328664